IMAGES
of America

WICHITA'S LEBANESE
HERITAGE

IMAGES
of America

WICHITA'S LEBANESE HERITAGE

Jay M. Price, Victoria Foth Sherry, Matthew Namee,
Raymond Crosse, and Andrea Schniepp Burgardt

ARCADIA
PUBLISHING

Published by Arcadia Publishing
Charleston, South Carolina

Library of Congress Control Number: 2009928537

For all general information contact Arcadia Publishing at:
Telephone 843-853-2070
Fax 843-853-0044
E-mail sales@arcadiapublishing.com
For customer service and orders:
Toll-Free 1-888-313-2665

Visit us on the Internet at www.arcadiapublishing.com

CONTENTS

ACKNOWLEDGMENTS

Books of this type are always team efforts. The project team appreciates all of the assistance that we have received from the staff of St. George Orthodox Christian Cathedral; St. Mary Orthodox Christian Church; the Kansas State Historical Society; Special Collections and University Archives, Wichita State University Libraries; the Wichita-Sedgwick County Historical Museum; and the *Wichita Eagle*. We would especially like to thank the Rt. Rev. Basil Essey, Bishop of Wichita and the Diocese of Mid-America, for his support and efforts. The people and families that provided the photographs, stories, artifacts, and advice are too numerous to name individually, although we are appreciative of each of their contributions. However, we would like to recognize Dr. Sam Cohlmia for his assistance in translating Arabic and advising us on the transliteration of Lebanese place names. We also want to say thank you to the many friends, family, colleagues, and students who have all been supportive and valuable sounding boards for this project. Finally thanks also goes to all the photographers, professional and amateur, who took the images that went into this book.

INTRODUCTION

Since arriving at the dawn of the 20th century, Lebanese Christians have participated actively in Wichita's entrepreneurial tradition. Although small in number, they have become among the city's best-known business families. They started as peddlers but quickly established themselves in groceries, tobacco, candy, and food wholesaling. At first, they were concentrated in the West Wichita neighborhood of Delano, but their influence ultimately extended across the city.

Under the influence of matriarchs and patriarchs, the Lebanese established deep roots in Wichita. Family connections included a network of relatives across southern Kansas and northern Oklahoma. They operated as extended clans, with adults, children, and various relatives living under one roof. Initially identifying themselves as Syrians, men and women organized St. George and St. Mary churches. They joined fraternal orders, participated in women's clubs, and, starting in the 1930s, organized clubs that promoted socializing and perpetuated Syrian traditions.

The years during and after World War II saw a shift in the fortunes and dynamics of the community. New generations branched out into new business ventures. Col. James Jabara brought nationwide attention to the Lebanese of Wichita as the first jet ace in the Korean conflict. Families began to leave Delano for other parts of town.

The latter decades of the 20th century have been times of change. Generations who came of age in the postwar years increasingly married non-Lebanese spouses. Some left the Orthodox faith while a steady stream of converts embraced Orthodox Christianity. Meanwhile tensions in Lebanon sent a new wave of emigrants to Wichita. The arrival of Lebanese Muslims added to the complexity of the Wichita scene.

Today the Lebanese presence is intertwined with Wichita life. Lebanese family names adorn the buildings at Wichita State University. The Lebanese dinners at St. George and St. Mary churches are popular local events. Despite being in the middle of beef country, Wichita restaurants commonly serve hummus appetizers and fattouch salad. Those who fly the Beechcrafts, Cessnas, and Learjets made in Wichita often travel in and out of Jabara Airport. From a handful of peddlers, the Lebanese have become among the city's most influential communities.

Jebran Shdeed and his wife, Khazna Abu Samra, stood outside their home in Ain Ebel, Lebanon, near Jedeidat Marjeyoun, around 1900. The couple typified the generation whose children sought a better life in America. Daughter Miriam (Mary) and her husband, Esa Razook, would travel to Kansas in 1906, farming in Cowley County before building a house in Wichita in 1918. (Courtesy Grace F. Barkett and Kansas State Historical Society.)

One

BORN ENTREPRENEURS

The Syrian immigrants who arrived in Wichita in the early 20th century were part of a larger exodus that brought 100,000 Lebanese Christians to the United States by 1920. Once the prosperous mercantile center of the Arab world, Syria's Lebanon region descended into poverty after disease ravaged its vineyards and Asian competition destroyed the silk trade. Under the weakening Ottoman Empire, tensions flared between Lebanon's religious factions. Muslim authorities increasingly subjected Christians to arbitrary persecution and military conscription. Syrian Christians seeking a better life turned to distant America as a proverbial "land of milk and honey," where "money grew on trees." Although poor, Syrian Lebanese immigrants shunned the factory and wage labor jobs that drew immigrants from Eastern Europe, preferring to go into business for themselves. Most began as peddlers, selling linens, lace, and needles from farm to farm and town to town. Always on the lookout for fresh territory, peddlers from southern Lebanon recognized opportunity in the burgeoning city of Wichita and its surrounding farms. By 1910, Wichita had become the supply hub for a network of 50 peddlers who crisscrossed Kansas and northern Oklahoma by foot or horse-drawn wagon. As they accumulated capital, peddlers moved into retail, opening stores and groceries in Wichita and along their former peddling routes. These entrepreneurs, in turn, brought relatives to Wichita to work in their stores and warehouses, establishing an enduring Lebanese presence.

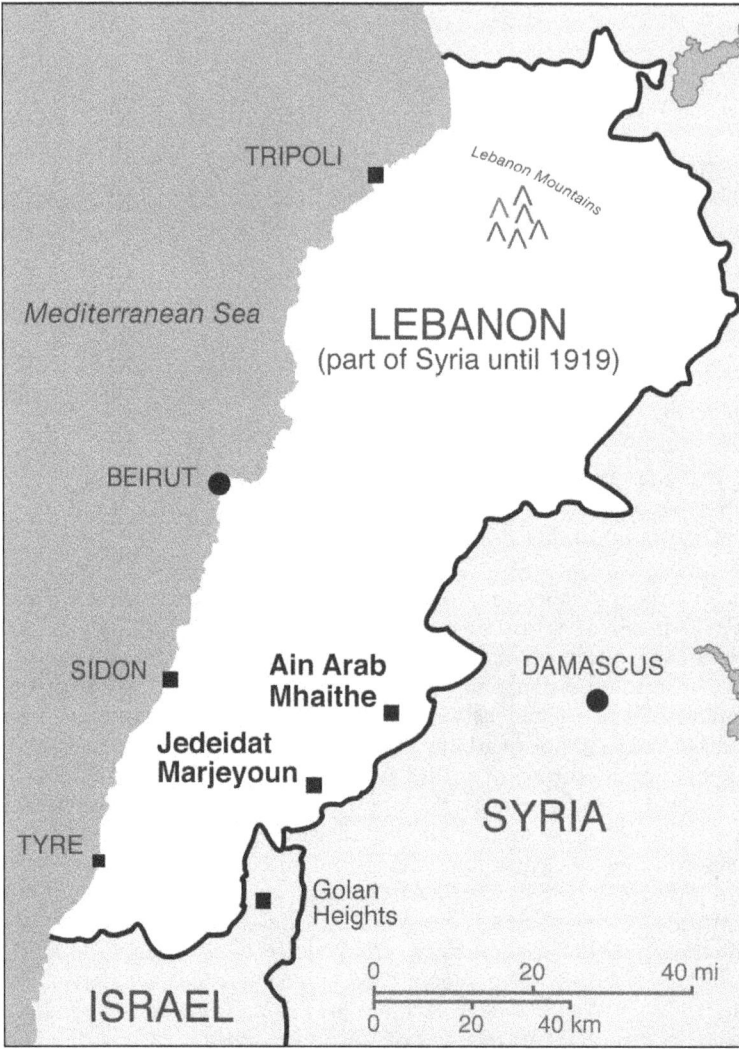

The Lebanese community in Wichita today traces its ancestry almost exclusively to three southern Lebanese villages: Jedeidat Marjeyoun, Mhaithe, and Ain Arab. Over many generations, the families residing in these villages became closely connected to each other through marriage and business ties. Once in Wichita, villagers sponsored family members and former neighbors to join them, replicating village ties in their new home.

Jedeidat Marjeyoun was the largest of the Lebanese villages whose residents settled in Wichita. A *Wichita Eagle* article in 1933 described Jedeidat as "one of the most entrancing valleys in the world . . . as rich to the eye as it is to the minds of historians." Early Jedeidat

Old timers said that it took longer to smoke a cigarette than it did to walk between the neighboring villages of Ain Arab (shown here in 1993) and Mhaithe. The early Mhaithe families in Wichita included the Stevenses, Namees, Wolfs, and Ferrises; the Kallail, Addis, and Solomon families were among those from Ain Arab. (Courtesy Kallail family and Kansas State Historical Society.)

families include the Farhas, Cohlmias, Bayouths, Ojiles, and Shadids. This 1923 photograph of Jedeidat was taken by M. G. Barkett. (Courtesy St. George Orthodox Cathedral and Kansas State Historical Society.)

Tensions between the many religious factions in Syria helped drive Lebanese Christians to emigrate. Although Muslims, Druze, and Christians often coexisted in relative peace and isolation under the Ottoman Empire, which had ruled Syria since the 1500s, sectarian violence increased as Ottoman power declined. Deeb Haddad and Touma Daher took up arms to defend their Christian village against the Druze around 1920. (Courtesy Kallail family.)

Some Lebanese men came to America to evade forced conscription into the Ottoman army. Frank Stevens, born in Mhaithe in 1895, fled his village and lived in the mountains for six years to avoid military service. He immigrated to Mexico in 1924 and made his way to Wichita, where he joined the Stevens family tobacco business. (Courtesy Eric Namee and Kansas State Historical Society.)

Father and sons wear traditional Arab clothing in this 1906 photograph of the Luthf and Halaya Diab family in Jedeidat Marjeyoun. France, Russia, and other European powers established schools and missions for Lebanese Christians in the late 19th century. These influences appear in the westernized attire of the young women, who immigrated to Oklahoma in 1913. (Courtesy Linda Shanbour and Kansas State Historical Society.)

Farhat (Frank) Ferris and his brother-in-law Saleem Namee (right) attended a wedding together in Mhaithe around 1900. The Ferris and Namee families both ended up in Wichita, where marriage ties between the families continued down the generations. (Courtesy Tracy Namee and Kansas State Historical Society.)

The young family of Farah Farha and Nahima Salamy Farha posed for the camera in 1913 in Jedeidat Marjeyoun. After her husband's death, Nahima and her children joined relatives in Wichita in the early 1920s. Within a few years the boys pictured here (Sam, Bahij, William, and infant La Bebe) went on to establish some of Wichita's most successful Lebanese enterprises. (Courtesy Grace F. Barkett and Kansas State Historical Society.)

Syrian immigrants arrived through many ports, including Ellis Island and Galveston. A few came to the United States via Canada and Mexico. Although most Syrians settled in the East or the industrial heartland, a few families made their way to the Great Plains. Those who came to Wichita likely first saw the city from the platform of one of Wichita's several railroad stations, such as the Santa Fe, above, or the Rock Island, below. Rail lines later enabled peddlers to travel to smaller towns where they made their rounds. (Above courtesy Wichita-Sedgwick County Historical Museum; below, courtesy Grant Hewitt.)

Joseph Namee peddled clothing and notions from the back of his horse-drawn wagon until 1913 in Worcester, Massachusetts. The earliest Lebanese immigrants often began life in North America as peddlers. Like many peddlers, Namee soon accumulated enough capital to transition to the dry goods business. After his move to Wichita in 1928, he hit the road again for a few years as a traveling tobacco salesman. (Courtesy Sadie Namee.)

Peddler Sim'aan (Samuel) Ayesh of Wichita used this portable cast iron tie ring to secure his horse while calling on customers. (Courtesy Richard Ayesh, photograph by Jay M. Price.)

16

Nemetallah Faris (N. F.) Farha built up the Lebanese population in Wichita by sponsoring the immigration of dozens of relatives and neighbors from his native village of Jedeidat Marjeyoun. He immigrated to the United States in 1895, peddling in Illinois and Oklahoma before arriving in Wichita in 1898. By 1910, he supplied wholesale merchandise to 50 free agents, both men and women, who shared with him the profits from their peddling routes in Kansas and Oklahoma. When he married Nabiha Bayouth in 1906, the wedding invitation was printed in English and Arabic. (Courtesy Marlene Samra Orr and Kansas State Historical Society.)

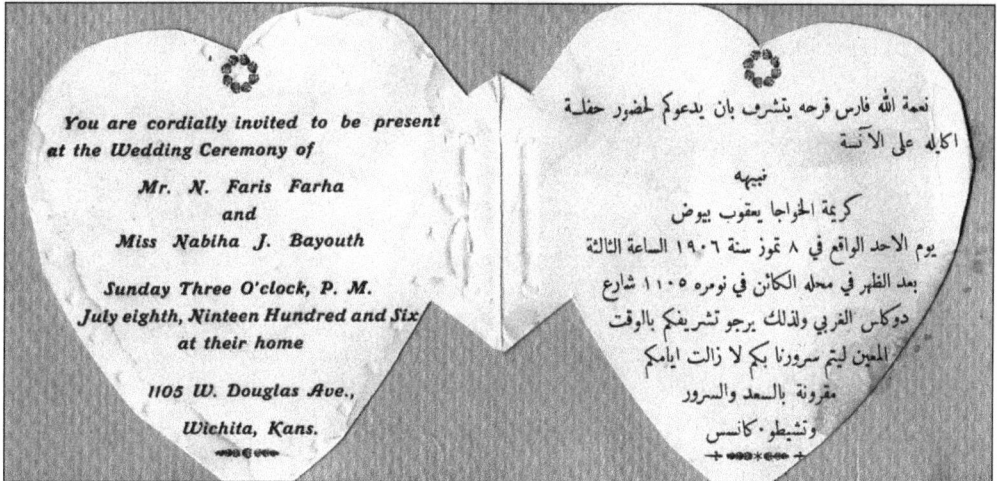

You are cordially invited to be present at the Wedding Ceremony of

Mr. N. Faris Farha
and
Miss Nabiha J. Bayouth

Sunday Three O'clock, P. M.
July eighth, Ninteen Hundred and Six
at their home

1105 W. Douglas Ave.,
Wichita, Kans.

نعمة الله فارس فرحه يتشرف بان يدعوكم لحضور حفلة
اكليله على الآنسة

نبيهه
كريمة الخواجا يعقوب بيوض
يوم الاحد الواقع في ٨ تموز سنة ١٩٠٦ الساعة الثالثة
بعد الظهر في محله الكائن في نمره ١١٠٥ شارع
دوكلاس الغربي ولذلك يرجو تشريفكم بالوقت
المعين ليتم سرورنا بكم لا زالت ايامكم
مقرونة بالسعد والسرور
وتشيطو . كانس

Born in Illinois in 1893, Sam Kallail arrived in Oklahoma in 1907. Three years later, at age 16, he had already acquired this "commercial wagon" to peddle goods from town to town. His success as a traveling salesman enabled him to open a dry goods store on the main street of Towanda, Kansas, in 1919. (Courtesy Kallail family and Kansas State Historical Society.)

Farris George Jabara, shown in his peddler's wagon, came to the United States in 1903, initially going to Texas and later to Oklahoma. In time, Jabara migrated to Kansas, establishing a grocery store in the Cowley County town of Burden. (Courtesy Fran Jabara.)

Jabour Swyd (George) Ablah resided in Wichita, but rode the train each Monday morning to Florence, Kansas, where he kept a horse and buggy to sell his wares to housewives in the vicinity. Ablah appears here with wife Hushfa (Nellie), daughter Hasseba, and sons Fauzie (Frank) and Hafiz (Harvey). He opened a dry goods store in 1907, ending his peddling career. (Courtesy Lindy Andeel.)

Shurkry Bayouth came to Kansas in 1912 with a passion for creating sesame-based products that he hoped would make him the George Washington Carver of sesame seeds. He boasted that a sesame plant grew in his Wichita driveway, demonstrating how hardy the plant was. (Courtesy Michael and Julia Bayouth.)

Sam and Clara Kallail stand proudly in front of their dry goods store in the small Butler County town of Towanda around 1919. Like many former peddlers, Kallail set up shop in one of the towns on his peddling route. By 1928, he had relocated his business to Wichita's Delano district, where his father and brother also ran a grocery. (Courtesy Kallail family and Kansas State Historical Society.)

Farris (F. A.), Sam, and W. A. Razook were brothers who arrived in Kansas in 1901. W. A. became a merchant in Burden. F. A. and Sam Razook operated a store in Cambridge for a time. In 1915, the three bothers came together to operate this general mercantile store in Moundridge. Later on, Sam established a store in Hesston. (Courtesy Gene Razook.)

Neman (N. S.) Farha established this 1908 storefront in Wichita's Lassen Hotel, advertising as a "dealer in art goods, Persian rugs, linens, and laces." He had arrived in Wichita eight years earlier under the sponsorship of cousin N. F. Farha and peddled between Wichita and Tulsa. In time, N. F.'s family became known as "the big family," while N. S.'s descendants were "the little family." (Courtesy Warren Farha and Kansas State Historical Society.)

Ellis Bayouth arrived in Wichita in 1906 and by 1915 owned this grocery on West Douglas. In those days, the store clerk jotted down in Arabic his customer's order. Then he collected the goods from store shelves and sometimes even delivered them to the customer's home. Bartering for merchandise was an accepted practice, but stores discouraged credit. (Courtesy Robert E. Bayouth and Kansas State Historical Society.)

Ellis George (E. G.) Stevens and his brother Joseph established their first store in Las Animas, Colorado. A few years after Joseph's death in 1913, E. G. married his brother's widow, Hundumie, came to Wichita, and entered the wholesale tobacco business. He became one of the most successful Lebanese merchants in the city and the patriarch of the Mhaithe community. The family operated Air Capital Tobacco Company until the 1980s. (Above, courtesy Eric and Tracy Namee and Kansas State Historical Society; below, courtesy Don Stephan.)

Frank and Harvey Ablah came to Wichita in 1907 and worked in their father's dry goods business. By the 1920s, they had ventured into restaurant supply, along with rental properties. Financial success enabled Frank to purchase this automobile. (Courtesy Wichita-Sedgwick County Historical Museum.)

Although grocers and wholesalers predominated, a few Lebanese immigrants pursued the restaurant trade. The Variety Grill, located at 806 North Broadway, was started by Zikey G. Razook. In 1938, the Syrian City Directory of Wichita also advertised Jack Sifri's Sanitary Lunch and the Farris Barbecue, run by Jim Farris at 503 South Bluff Street. (Courtesy Gene Razook.)

23

Syrian merchants who originally supplied networks of peddlers often made the transition to the wholesale grocery business. The Farha brothers purchased F&E (Farha and Elkouri) Wholesale from an uncle in the 1920s and transformed it into Wichita's largest and most enduring Lebanese wholesale grocery enterprise. (Courtesy Wichita-Sedgwick County Historical Museum.)

The Ablah brothers' wholesale food business operated for many years from this location at 205 North Water Street. Early on, the company became a pioneer in the emerging fast food industry, working with the newly founded White Castle hamburger chain. (Courtesy Wichita-Sedgwick County Historical Museum.)

The neighborhood west of the Arkansas River became the center for Lebanese families and businesses. Called Delano or West Wichita, the area inherited a tawdry reputation from its 1870s cowtown days of saloons and brothels. The main intersection at the lower left is Seneca Street and West Douglas Avenue. Along Douglas Avenue, merchants such as E. G. Stevens, Frank Ferris, E. N. Laham, Ellis Bayouth, and Zack Farha, among others, operated businesses. Family homes stood north and south of Douglas, in the tree-covered areas. (Courtesy Special Collections and University Archives, Wichita State University Libraries.)

Ellis Bayouth stands in front of his second grocery, at 1200 West Douglas Avenue, in 1922; below, the store interior is seen six years later. Bayouth's wife, Zakia, and children clerked in the store. In later years, the Bayouth sons opened groceries at several locations throughout the city, but the Delano store remained a Wichita fixture until it closed in 1996. Ellis was one of the first Wichita merchants to offer his customers 24-hour shopping, dozing in a chair and getting up whenever a shopper arrived. (Courtesy Robert E. Bayouth and Kansas State Historical Society.)

Oscar Kallail followed his father, Joseph, and brother Sam into retail trade, operating the O. K. Grocery on West Douglas Avenue. Father, sons, and sister Lasema, shown here around 1925, all clerked in the store. (Courtesy Kallail family and Kansas State Historical Society.)

After their arranged marriage in 1931, Taft and Julia Stevens Stephan ran several groceries in Wichita. They lived in the back of a store at the time of the birth of their first son, Robert. An entrepreneur in her own right, Julia later acquired the Kibbe Grocery at Third Street and Meridian Avenue and started Stephan Variety Store that "had more buttons than Woolworth's." (Courtesy Don Stephan.)

The Farha brothers opened their first Cut Rate Foods store in 1928 and operated at three locations by the time of this 1935 photograph. The earliest discount grocery chain in Wichita, Cut Rate pioneered the concept of low prices combined with self-service shopping. These innovations proved highly popular with Depression-era consumers. Both Lebanese immigrants and the first-born American generation staffed the stores as clerks, bookkeepers, and cashiers. (Courtesy Warren Farha and Kansas State Historical Society.)

With his tobacco warehouse, traveling salesmen, and fleet of delivery trucks, E. G. Stevens became the other major employer in the Lebanese community. Old country village and family ties were reinforced in Wichita's Lebanese businesses. Stevens generally hired workers from Mhaithe and Ain Arab, while those from Jedeidat Marjeyoun were likely to work for Cut Rate Foods or F&E Wholesale, the Farha enterprises. (Courtesy Keith Stevens.)

E. G. Stevens's cousin, David Stevens, followed him into the tobacco and candy wholesale trade in 1932. In typical Lebanese fashion, he relied on extended family to develop the D. Stevens Candy Company with the motto "a wholesale store to your door." Nephew Keeney's son, Keith, appears at right with David and Mary, who had no children of their own. (Courtesy Keith Stevens.)

Lebanese women who took over the family business as widows or divorcees proved themselves capable businesswomen. Lizzie Henry emigrated from Ain Arab at age 11 and opened a market on South Seneca Street in 1920 with her husband John (Hanna El Assais). Widowed in 1932, Lizzie and her children ran the store until 1949. She earned a reputation as a shrewd proprietor. (Courtesy Kallail family.)

Sadie Shanbour lost her husband in 1933, three weeks after the birth of their youngest son. With family assistance, she moved into a combined house and storefront in Wichita that rented for $50 a month. "It was three steps from the store into our home, so my mother could keep an eye on the kids and support us at the same time," recalled her son. (Courtesy Mitchell Shanbour and Kansas State Historical Society.)

Rose Farris, left, operated a general store in Ashland, Kansas, with her husband, John. The couple opened the Farris Market in Wichita during the Depression, with Rose managing the store after her husband's death. Their daughter, Lillie, center, ran an Ashland grocery with husband Ellis Cohlmia. After she was widowed, Lillie followed her mother to Wichita and started Lillie's, a clothing store for children. (Courtesy Bob Razook.)

Sadie Wolf received the family grocery store in Wichita as part of the settlement in her divorce from Joseph Wolf in the 1920s. A native of Damascus, Sadie was one of the first Syrian women in Wichita to assume the role of sole proprietor. Reportedly, she expressed her opinion of her ex-husband by throwing eggs at his car when he was in the vicinity. (Courtesy Mary Ann Khoury.)

In the 1920s, Najeeb (George) Shadid became one of first Syrian entrepreneurs to locate his business outside the Delano district. North of downtown Wichita, the Shadid Super Market catered to an African American clientele. His wife, Marina Kallail, came from Ain Arab, while Shadid was a Jedeidat native. (Courtesy Kallail family.)

Over the years, other Lebanese businesses served the African American community. Among them was Jim Elkouri's Stop and Shop at 13th Street and Indiana Avenue. (Courtesy Grant Hewitt.)

In 1930, Tenaal "Tiny" Farha operated this grocery in Coffeyville in southeast Kansas. Lebanese-run stores were common across southern Kansas and northern Oklahoma during the prosperous 1920s. The Great Depression forced many small town proprietors out of business and some went to work for relatives in Wichita. This trend continued in the postwar years as Kansas's rural economy gradually declined. (Courtesy Alfred Farha and Kansas State Historical Society.)

The fates of Lebanese businesses outside of Wichita often mirrored the rise and fall of local economies. Established during the heyday of small town life, stores such as Razook's in Moundridge participated in local events and festivities, including this parade. The downturn of the 1930s put the Razook store out of business and prompted the family to move to Wichita. (Courtesy Gene Razook.)

After 1924, immigration from Syria virtually ended, but an influx from the Midwest and East Coast helped double the size of Wichita's Lebanese population from 1928 to 1938. The Lahams first operated a store in Norfolk, Nebraska. Seeking greater Lebanese contact, the family chose Wichita over Chicago, reportedly in a coin toss. In 1938, Thomas Laham's new store advertised gloves, hosiery, and other luxuries. (Courtesy Thomas Laham.)

Adeeb E. Andeel and his family spent the 1920s following the oil strikes across Oklahoma before coming to Wichita, where he set up and maintained vending machines. This photograph shows Andeel with his son, daughter, and Ablah in-laws. (Courtesy Lindy Andeel.)

John Jabara, shown with his wife and children in a later photograph, settled in Wichita in the 1930s. Son James, center, became a decorated war hero and one of the most famous members of Wichita's Lebanese community. This branch of the family, like that of Burden merchant Farris Jabara, went by "Ja-BEAR-a," unlike the "Ja-BAHR-a" of other branches. (Courtesy Bob Razook.)

سِفْرُ الأَمْثَالِ

الفَصْلُ الأَوَّلُ

أَمْثَالُ سُلَيْمَانَ بْنِ دَاوُدَ مَلِكِ إِسْرَائِيلَ. لِمَعْرِفَةِ الحِكْمَةِ وَالتَّأْدِيبِ. لِتَفَطُّنٍ لأَقْوَالِ الفِطْنَةِ. لِقَبُولِ تَأْدِيبِ التَّعَقُّلِ وَالعَدْلِ وَالحَقِّ وَالاسْتِقَامَةِ. لِتُعْطَى الأَغْمَارَ ذَكَاءً وَالحَدَثَ عِلْماً وَتَدَبُّراً. يَسْمَعُهَا الحَكِيمُ فَيَزْدَادُ عِلْماً وَالفَهِيمُ يَكْتَسِبُ تَدَابِيرَ. لِتَفَطُّنٍ لِمَثَلٍ وَلُغْزٍ أَقْوَالِ الحُكَمَاءِ وَغَوَامِضِهِمْ. مَخَافَةُ الرَّبِّ رَأْسُ العِلْمِ. أَمَّا الجَاهِلُونَ فَيَحْتَقِرُونَ الحِكْمَةَ وَالأَدَبَ. اِسْمَعْ يَا ابْنِي تَأْدِيبَ أَبِيكَ وَلاَ تَرْفُضْ شَرِيعَةَ أُمِّكَ. لأَنَّهُمَا إِكْلِيلُ نِعْمَةٍ لِرَأْسِكَ وَقَلاَئِدُ لِعُنُقِكَ. يَا ابْنِي إِنْ تَمَلَّقَكَ الخُطَاةُ فَلاَ تَرْضَخْ. إِنْ قَالُوا هَلُمَّ مَعَنَا لِنَكْمُنْ لِلدَّمِ لِنَخْتَفِ لِلْبَرِيءِ بَاطِلاً. لِنَبْتَلِعْهُمْ أَحْيَاءً كَالهَاوِيَةِ وَصِحَاحاً كَالهَابِطِينَ فِي الجُبِّ. فَنَجِدَ كُلَّ مَالٍ نَفِيسٍ نَمْلَأُ بُيُوتَنَا غَنِيمَةً. تُلْقِي قُرْعَتَكَ وَسْطَنَا وَيَكُونُ لَنَا جَمِيعاً كِيسٌ وَاحِدٌ. يَا ابْنِي لاَ تَسِرْ فِي الطَّرِيقِ مَعَهُمْ. اِمْنَعْ رِجْلَكَ عَنْ مَسَالِكِهِمْ. لأَنَّ أَقْدَامَهُمْ تَجْرِي إِلَى الشَّرِّ وَتُسْرِعُ إِلَى سَفْكِ الدَّمِ. لأَنَّهُ بَاطِلاً تُنْصَبُ الشَّبَكَةُ أَمَامَ عَيْنَيْ كُلِّ ذِي جَنَاحٍ. أَمَّا هُمْ فَيَكْمُنُونَ

Christianity spread rapidly through the Middle East in the first century after Christ. Arab Christians were numerous in Syria and Lebanon even after the rise of Islam. These Christian communities enjoyed protection and considerable autonomy under various Muslim empires, including the Ottomans. Lebanese Christians who immigrated to Wichita brought with them prayer books and Bibles in Arabic. This Bible, opened to the Book of Proverbs, belonged to Samuel and Mabel Ayesh. (Courtesy Richard Ayesh.)

Raised in the environs of the Holy Land, many Orthodox Christians in the Middle East experienced their ancient faith as a living spiritual reality. Some Wichita descendants of Lebanese immigrants recall parents and grandparents describing visits from saints or angels. The Ferris family preserves stories of ancestor Ferris Haddad, a local holy man who preached to fellow villagers from the rooftops of Mhaithe. According to legend, an angel foretold his death. (Courtesy Evelyn Ferris.)

Two

BONDS OF
FAITH AND FAMILY

Lebanon remained part of Syria until the Ottoman Empire's collapse at the end of World War I. The new state functioned as a French mandate for two decades, achieving independence only in the 1940s. Religious affiliation has always defined Lebanese identity to a far greater degree than nationality. The Ottoman millet system, while favoring Muslims, afforded other faith groups a degree of self-governance that reinforced religious loyalties. The Christian majority in Lebanon was itself divided between the Maronites and Melkites (Byzantine Rite Catholics) and the Orthodox, who occupied the lowest rung of the Ottoman hierarchy. Not surprisingly, the vast majority of Lebanese who immigrated to America belonged to this latter group, although some Roman Catholics came as well. In Wichita, visiting Orthodox clergy began performing weddings and baptisms for the city's Lebanese immigrants as early as 1903. Once or twice a year, a traveling priest celebrated the Eucharist, often in the living room of a private home. In 1918, Lebanese immigrants founded the city's first Orthodox church, St. George, located in the heart of the Lebanese neighborhood in West Wichita. A second church, St. Mary, began in 1932. The Orthodox Church served as the focal point of community life as the Lebanese presence in Wichita grew steadily through marriages, births, and the arrival of relatives from Lebanon and other U.S. cities.

Many Lebanese immigrants to Wichita came from Jedeidat Marjeyoun, where they attended St. George Orthodox Church. The Orthodox Church is the predominant expression of Christianity in the East, including Russia, Greece, and the Arab world. Orthodox bishops trace their unbroken line of succession back to the apostles. Orthodox liturgy, theology, and traditions have changed little over the centuries. (Courtesy Chris Razook.)

There were neither Orthodox churches nor clergy in Wichita for the first two decades of the 20th century. Fr. Nicola Yanney, assigned to St. George Syrian Orthodox Church in Kearney, Nebraska, made occasional trips to Wichita to perform baptisms and celebrate the Divine Liturgy. Fr. Nicola encouraged the Lebanese community to establish the city's first Orthodox Christian church. (Courtesy Rt. Rev. Basil Essey and Kansas State Historical Society.)

The immigrant community in 1918 purchased this wooden building on Handley Street in the heart of the Syrian neighborhood, converting it into the city's first Orthodox church. Despite its lack of space and amenities, St. George quickly became the focal point of community life. (Courtesy Mary Razook.)

Parishioners gathered outside St. George for the funeral procession for Fr. George Cohlmia in 1947. The modern American clothing of the lay people contrasts with the ornate ceremonial robes of the altar servers and clergy. (Courtesy Wichita-Sedgwick County Historical Museum.)

Prior to coming to the United States, Rt. Rev. Economos Shukrallah Shadid served the parish in Marjeyoun. He pastored St. Elijah Orthodox Church in Oklahoma City and conducted services in Wichita whenever its church was without a priest. St. George's governing board incorporated under his guidance in 1921. Orthodox parish priests are usually married, and Fr. Shukrallah and his wife raised a large family. Several descendants reside in Wichita today. A great-grandson and a great-nephew were ordained to the priesthood in Wichita in recent years. (Courtesy Linda Shanbour and Kansas State Historical Society.)

Along with religious faith, extended families formed a cornerstone of Lebanese culture. The itinerant nature of peddling, however, meant that the earliest arrivals in Wichita were mostly young, unmarried men. An exception was the Jacob and Saleema Bayouth family, who immigrated to Wichita in 1906, accompanied by their children and at least one relative. (Courtesy Wichita-Sedgwick Country Historical Museum.)

Once a Syrian immigrant established his livelihood, he often returned to the village in Lebanon to find a wife. Matches were usually arranged by parents or uncles, with marriages between distant cousins encouraged. After opening his art goods store in Wichita, N. S. Farha returned to Jedeidat in 1913 to marry Rose Diban and bring her to Kansas. (Courtesy Florence Vandervort and Kansas State Historical Society.)

In search of a suitable Lebanese wife, Joseph Namee traveled all the way from Massachusetts to Beaver, Oklahoma, where countryman Joseph Kallail ran a dry goods store. Kallail's daughters were born in Ain Arab, near Namee's native Mhaithe. When the first daughter, Lasema, turned down Namee's proposal of marriage, he asked her sister Saleemy (Thelma). She accepted and they were married in 1925. The couple moved to Wichita and operated a grocery store together for many years. (Courtesy Eric and Tracy Namee and Kansas State Historical Society.)

Lebanese wedding celebrations could last a week or longer, and doubled as occasions for joyous family and village reunions. Relatives traveled from Wichita, Oklahoma City, and surrounding towns to attend this 1928 wedding in Osawatomie, Kansas. Newlyweds Henry and Saada Zakoura Farha took up residence in Wichita. (Courtesy Robert E. Bayouth and Kansas State Historical Society.)

Displays of affection remain common in Middle Eastern cultures, implying a deep bond that often involved familial as well as personal ties. As emigration from Syria unfolded, however, family ties became more difficult to maintain. Shurkry Bayouth, right, settled in Wichita, while his brother-in-law went to South America, another favored destination for Syrian emigrants. (Courtesy Michael and Julia Bayouth.)

Elizabeth Solomon married Ray Shadid in
1917 in Wellington, Kansas. Many brides
and grooms met only a few times before their
wedding, yet harmonious marriages lasting for
decades were common. "My parents thought
he was a good boy," said Jamelia Najim of
the husband she married in 1933 after two
months' acquaintance. "And I was sure my
parents wouldn't mislead me." (Courtesy Mary
Shadid and Kansas State Historical Society.)

Hasseba Ablah, Frank and Harvey Ablah's sister, married Adeeb Andeel in 1922. Informal
business connections between the Ablahs and the Andeels have continued down through the
generations. (Courtesy Lindy Andeel.)

One striking aspect of Lebanese home life was the preference for extended family living arrangements. Adult children typically lived with parents, even after they married and had children of their own. All of Nahima Farha's adult children shared their mother's Riverside home at various times throughout the 1930s and 1940s, while the others lived nearby. Several grandchildren were born there. (Courtesy Betty Aboussie Ellis.)

Nuclear family living arrangements became more common starting in the 1930s, but the patriarch remained the head of the family. E. G. and Hundumie Stevens gathered in front of the home where they lived with their three young sons, dressed in white shirts. Joining them are Hundumie's sons and daughter from her first marriage, their spouses, and E. G.'s sister Mary and brother Frank (both far left). (Courtesy Eric and Tracy Namee.)

46

Syrian immigrants worshipped together at St. George for 14 years until the community split, reportedly over a building dispute. Led by E. G. Stevens, several men formed the Society of St. Mary American-Syrian Orthodox Church in 1932. Mhaithe and Ain Arab families joined St. Mary, while most Jedeidat families continued to worship at St. George. (Courtesy Wichita-Sedgwick County Historical Museum.)

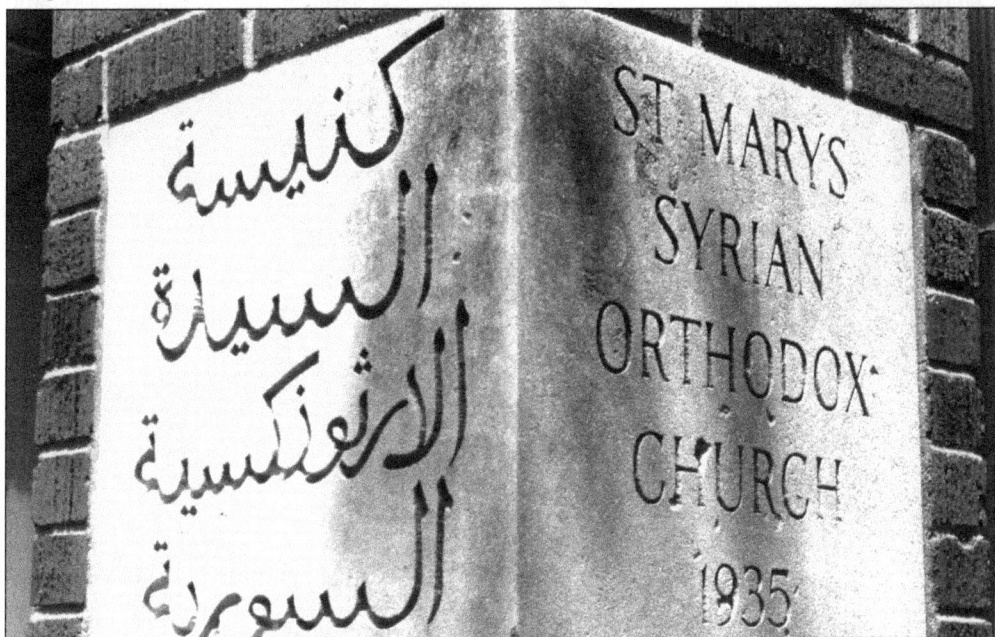

The cornerstone of St. Mary, featuring both Arabic and English script, illustrates the founders' dual identity as Syrians and Americans. A time capsule in the cornerstone contained copies of Wichita newspapers and Arabic periodicals. When the time capsule was opened decades later, almost none of the founders' descendants knew enough Arabic to read the latter. (Courtesy Rosemary Kallail and Kansas State Historical Society.)

The interior of St. Mary's, shown here in the 1950s, displayed features typical of Orthodox Christian worship: crosses, vigil lamps, and an iconostasis (icon screen) separating the church nave from the altar. Icons of Jesus, the Theotokos (Virgin Mary), Archangels Michael and Gabriel, the Mystical (Last) Supper, the apostles, and other saints faced the congregation and served as aids to prayer. (Courtesy Keith Stevens.)

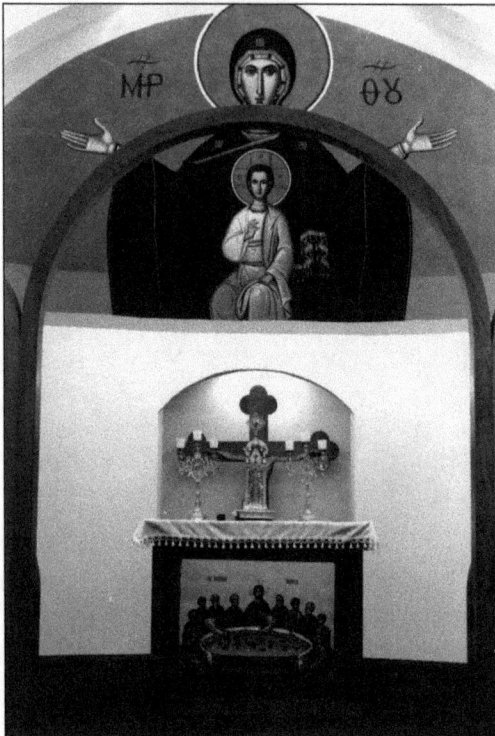

Parish leaders commissioned these icons of the Theotokos and the Mystical Supper for the altar area in 1980. Church furnishings were often donated as family memorials or, like the crucifix behind the altar, hand crafted by a St. Mary parishioner. (Photograph by Sam Namee, courtesy Eric Namee.)

The chronic shortage of Syrian
Orthodox clergy in America
meant that Wichita was often
without a priest in the 1920s and
early 1930s. Some pious Syrian
men left secular life to enter the
priesthood. One was Fr. Nicholas
Husson, a former carpenter who
shepherded St. Mary Orthodox
Church from 1941 to 1946.
(Courtesy Lorraine Ferris and
Kansas State Historical Society.)

Fr. George Cohlmia entered the
priesthood in 1933 in order to pastor
St. George Orthodox Church, where he
served until his death in 1947. (Courtesy
Jean Cohlmia.)

Wichita's Lebanese community gathered in 1936 to honor a visiting bishop from southern Lebanon. Metropolitan Theodosius Abourjaily, whose diocese of Tyre and Sidon included Jedaidat Marjeyoun, was later elected Patriarch of Antioch. One of the five ancient sees of Christianity, Antioch maintains jurisdiction over the churches of Syria, Lebanon, and the Syrian diaspora in the Americas. (Courtesy Mary Razook.)

Fr. George Cohlmia brought Metropolitan Theodosius to Ashland, Kansas, home of his relatives Ellis and Lillie Cohlmia. Members of the extended Cohlmia clan descended on tiny Ashland, some 170 miles west of Wichita, for the occasion. (Courtesy Dr. Sam Cohlmia.)

In 1948, the St. George parish built a new church at Walnut and Texas Streets. Still in the heart of the old Syrian neighborhood, the new building accommodated a growing congregation. The first services took place on Christmas Eve 1948 in the parish hall, with the sanctuary first used on Pascha (Easter) in 1949. (Courtesy Wichita-Sedgwick County Historical Museum.)

The matriarchs of St. George gathered on the steps of the new church with Fr. John Matthiesen, who served from 1950 until 1963. These Lebanese mothers and grandmothers played an instrumental role in raising funds to build and maintain the new church and assumed primary responsibility for passing the Orthodox faith on to the next generation. (Courtesy Mary Razook.)

The 1930s and 1940s saw Wichita's Syrian immigrants refining their new American identity, even as they carried on cultural traditions rooted in Lebanon. For the first generation born in America, lasting bonds with childhood companions provided a sense of security and belonging as they came of age in an increasingly individualistic world. Ray Stevens and Eli Ferris remained lifelong friends of their cousins Ernest and Sam Namee. (Courtesy Eric and Tracy Namee.)

Three

NAVIGATING IDENTITY AND COMMUNITY

By 1938, Wichita's Syrian-Lebanese community had grown to around 115 households whose members moved within the tight-knit circles of church, neighborhood, and family. From the beginning, however, the immigrants made connections within the larger sphere of Wichita society. Merchants joined the Masons and other fraternal orders to facilitate contacts with local businessmen. Arabic might have been the language spoken at home and church, but clerks, salespeople, and waiters rapidly became conversant in English, as did children growing up in this bi-cultural world. Within a few years of arriving in America, most Syrians applied for U.S. citizenship and spoke proudly of their patriotism. A handful of men enlisted during World War I, and the response to Pearl Harbor was overwhelming: virtually every Wichita family sent one or more sons off to war. In keeping with old country custom, women worked alongside husbands and fathers in the family business but seldom socialized outside the home. Such traditions changed gradually with the emergence of Lebanese social clubs and the inauguration of annual fundraising dinners that introduced Wichitans to Lebanese cuisine. Wichitans, in turn, were slow to fully accept the newcomers in their midst. The olive-skinned Lebanese endured racial slurs, and even wealthy families such as the Farhas and Stevenses could not join the Wichita Country Club.

Fraternal lodges flourished in the early 20th century. Lodge membership cemented one's standing within the local business community. Syrian immigrants like Joseph Deeb Wolf joined lodges to broaden their network of social and commercial contacts. Many fraternal orders engaged in charitable work, which appealed strongly to men steeped in Arab traditions of generosity and hospitality to strangers. (Courtesy Wichita-Sedgwick County Historical Museum.)

Sam Kallail joined the Masons within a few years of immigrating to Oklahoma and continued his affiliation after opening a dry goods store in Wichita. He wore his fez for this portrait with fellow Wichita storekeeper Ferris Jacob, proprietor of Jack's Market. (Courtesy Kallail family.)

Some early Syrian immigrants arrived in this country intending to return home within a few years, but the majority embraced their new homeland and quickly applied for citizenship. Sadie Shanbour's certificate verified that she became a citizen in 1902 at age eight, barely a year after her family set foot on American soil. At right are the naturalization papers of Jabour Ablah, whose family immigrated first to Canada. (Above, courtesy Mitchell and Linda Shanbour and Kansas State Historical Society; right, Courtesy Don Ablah.)

Arabic names such as Nemetallah and Ramze sounded strange to Americans; outside Lebanese circles, men often went by initials. Some adopted anglicizations: Menahe Razook became Minnie, and Wakeem Wehby became Charles. Last names presented yet another challenge. Lee and Ellis Cohlmia (above) altered their surname from the foreign-sounding "Ghulmeiah," and an Ellis Island mix-up left a branch of the same family with the name "Farris." (Courtesy Ruth Cohlmia.)

The tombstone of early Wichita immigrant Jacob Bayouth reveals the persistence of Arabic. Families spoke Arabic at home, but by the early 1930s, Syrian American newspapers lamented that the younger generation refused to master their parents' native tongue. "If we were out on the street and my mother and aunts started jibbering in Arabic, I felt so embarrassed," explained Marguerite Farha, born in 1914. (Photograph by Jay M. Price.)

Service in the armed forces was an important token of immigrant patriotism. As a young man, George Yusef Abla fought for the United States in World War I, the conflict that helped topple the Ottoman Empire and resulted in the separation of Lebanon from Syria. Abla returned to Lebanon after the war and married Alexandra Issa. The couple settled in Wichita in 1923. (Courtesy Jennie Abla and Kansas State Historical Society.)

Albert Zakoura proudly wears his World War I uniform. While serving overseas, he sent cards to his sisters back home in Osawatomie. After the war's end, he returned to Kansas to work in the family general store. (Courtesy Mitchell and Linda Shanbour and Kansas State Historical Society.)

Syrian immigrants adjusting to a new culture carefully crafted an "American" image that they projected to the world. This portrait of Frank and Mary Stevens Ferris with their four children around 1928 radiates a middle class decorum and respectability that belied Ferris's modest occupation. By contrast, his dramatic pose on this postcard, which conveyed Christmas greetings in Arabic, announces to fellow Syrians his triumphant arrival in Wichita and the environs of the great American West. (Courtesy Eric and Tracy Namee and Kansas State Historical Society.)

In the 1920s, the automobile gave ordinary city dwellers the means to enjoy the formerly elite American pastime of vacationing in the Rocky Mountains. The Bayouth and Cohlmia families made the trek to Monarch Pass in Colorado, photographing their adventures to signal that they now enjoyed a measure of the leisure time that success affords. (Courtesy Michael and Julia Bayouth.)

Fishing was among the most popular outdoor pursuits. Whether Ellis Cohlmia, right, and his gallant colleagues fished in their business suits, or were merely posing for the camera, is unknown. (Courtesy Bob Razook.)

Syrian women seldom socialized outside of family gatherings before the 1920s, when the Wichita Daughters of the American Revolution created the American Syrian Ladies Club. The club proposed to "promote friendship between the American and the Syrian women" of Wichita. For this 1923 photograph, several of the club's Syrian members donned their wedding dresses, the only fine clothing they owned. (Courtesy Florence Vandervort and Kansas State Historical Society.)

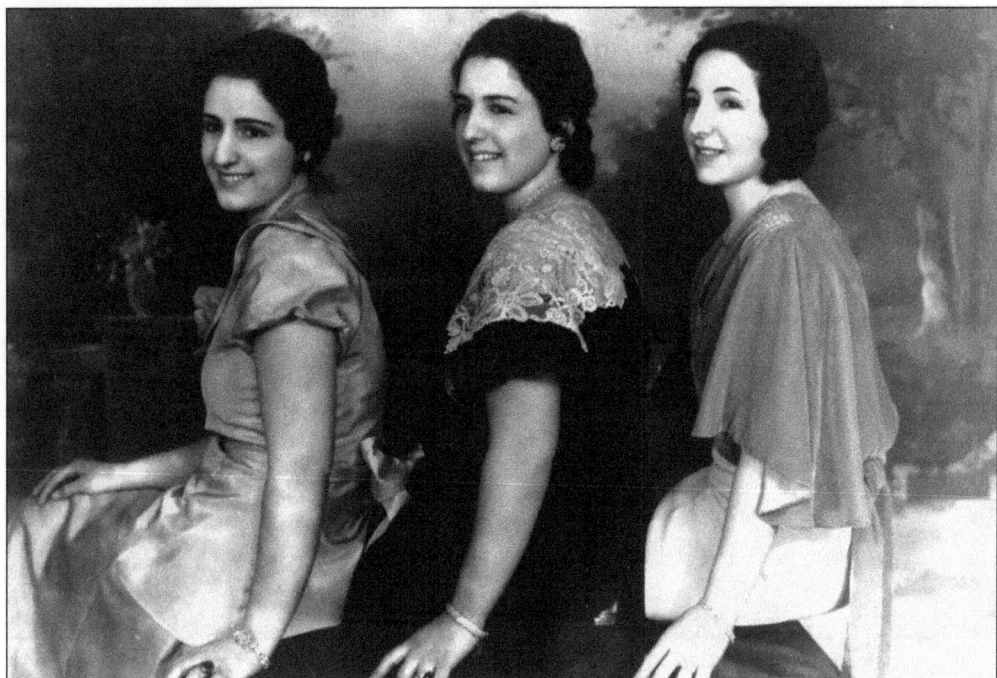

Victoria Farha, right, appears in her engagement dress with sisters Olga and Floreine. The *Wichita Eagle* published Victoria's engagement announcement, along with news of her 1930 election as financial secretary of the prestigious Wichita Federation of Women's Clubs. By the 1930s, the society pages regularly reported the activities of fashionable young Syrian women like the N. F. Farha daughters. (Courtesy Marlene Samra Orr and Kansas State Historical Society.)

In 1937, Charles Laham (shown as a Wichita University student around 1932) helped found Wichita's first secular Syrian organization. Composed of men and women of the American-born generation, the Al-pha Club devoted itself to "the welfare of our Syrian speaking people." The Al-phas organized the community's first Labor Day dance that year. In 1938, Laham spearheaded compilation of the first directory of Wichita's Syrian residents, businesses, and organizations. (Courtesy Thomas Laham.)

Club fever swept Wichita's Syrian youth starting in the late 1930s. At a birthday party in 1941, 13 teenage girls founded the Bona Dea Club "for Syrian girls only—and if a girl's afraid to be as ornery as we are, she can't join!" The Boneheads, as they affectionately called one another, have met bi-weekly in members' homes for over six decades. This ball took place in 1946. (Courtesy Bona Dea Club.)

Organized by the Bona Dea Club, this 1949 dance was held at the Broadview, one of Wichita's finest hotels. Club events of this era were elegant affairs, with formal gowns, well-dressed Lebanese escorts, and regular chaperones. Two bands were booked, one to play popular American swing tunes and the other, often a Syrian band from Texas, to accompany Arabic dances such as the dubke. (Courtesy Bona Dea Club.)

These young Syrian men started the Debonairs in the early 1940s. The club, whose name was chosen at random from the dictionary, disbanded while its members fought in World War II. After the war, the veterans came back together and formed the George David Lodge. Starting in 1947, lodge members assisted the Bona Dea Club in hosting the annual Labor Day dances for the Lebanese community. (Courtesy Richard Ayesh.)

Lambda Sigma Rho, started by older sisters and cousins of the Bona Dea members, organized many Labor Day festivities such as this baseball game between Lebanese teams from Oklahoma City and Wichita. The Lambda Sigs met for weekly card games well into the 1970s, and Wichitans knew better than to hold a funeral on a Tuesday night if they wanted Lambda Sig members to attend. (Courtesy Bona Dea Club.)

GREETINGS

We're Glad to See You!

THE LAMBDA SIGMA RHO

Welcomes You to the

BASEBALL GAME

OKLAHOMA CITY, OKLAHOMA

versus

WICHITA, KANSAS

Sunday, September 1, 1946

Lawrence Stadium Grounds

2 p. m.

CLUB ROSTER

PRESIDENT — Lucille Ablah
SECRETARY — Marie Ellis
TREASURER — Martha Stevens

Sally Bayouth	Mabel Laham
Louise Bazook Cohlmia	Ruth Addis Kamas
Blanche Farha	Lucille Moses
Anita Ferris	Mary Bazook Simon
Marybelle Elkouri Jabara	Julia Steven
Katherine David Elkouri	Esther Steven
	Lela Wehby

DANCE CHAIRMAN — Rose Farha

Wichita sent 100 of its young Lebanese American men to serve in various branches of the armed forces during World War II. Among those who saw action in Europe was George Laham, pictured with members of his U.S. Army unit. (Courtesy Marla Laham and Kansas State Historical Society.)

Fred Shanbour came of age just in time to serve in the U.S. Navy. (Courtesy Mitchell Shanbour and Kansas State Historical Society.)

George David was the only Lebanese soldier from Wichita who did not return from World War II. He lost his life at the Battle of the Bulge. After the war, Lebanese veterans named their social club the George David Lodge in his honor. (Courtesy Wichita-Sedgwick County Historical Museum.)

Many soldiers returned home as decorated war heroes. George Kallail earned the Silver Star for combat in France. (Courtesy Kallail family and Kansas State Historical Society.)

Dick Ayesh (center, in military jacket) built planes for Cessna at the outbreak of the war but longed to fly himself. He joined the U.S. Army Air Corps in 1943, participating in risky bombing missions over Germany near the war's end. Upon returning home a decorated lieutenant, he gathered with boyhood friends fresh from stints in the infantry, U.S. Air Force, U.S. Coast Guard, and Merchant Marine. (Courtesy Richard Ayesh.)

When Johnny Jabara, second from the left, came home from World War II, the Andeels drove out to meet him in San Francisco. (Courtesy Lindy Andeel.)

After the war, the Lebanese did not find themselves welcomed everywhere. Like Jews and African Americans, Arabs were barred from the Wichita Country Club. In response, Frank Solomon and Kenneth Razook (right, with VFW golf trophy) helped found the Rolling Hills Country Club in 1948. (Courtesy Bob Razook.)

The new club opened its doors to all Wichita residents. Over the years, Lebanese businessmen hosted several celebrity benefit golf tournaments at Rolling Hills in support of Wichita charities. (Photograph by Jay M. Price.)

The war years solidified perceptions of Wichita's Lebanese citizens as loyal Americans, but they also marked changes in Lebanese customs surrounding courtship and marriage. A modern Lebanese girl no longer needed a dowry or matchmakers in order to marry. These Syrian gold coins, part of Miriam Razook's dowry in the early 1900s, became a high school graduation bracelet for granddaughter Grace Farha in 1951. (Courtesy Grace F. Barkett and Heartland Orthodox Christian Museum.)

Going to war, to college, or to work outside the family business, young people increasingly forged social ties beyond the Lebanese community. To help youth find eligible marriage partners, Lebanese social gatherings such as this one occurred more frequently during the postwar years. Labor Day dances, the St. Mary Mahrajans, and church conventions introduced young people to their counterparts from other cities, resulting in many matches. (Courtesy Michael and Julia Bayouth.)

The Vivianne Bayouth and Fred Farha wedding took place in 1953 at St. George Orthodox Church. Marriages within the Lebanese community remained common, but by the 1950s and 1960s they were no longer the norm. During those decades, one out of every two weddings at St. George united a Lebanese bride or groom with a spouse of a different ethnic background. (Courtesy Marlene Samra Orr and Kansas State Historical Society.)

Bus Farha married Ruth Hudsonpillar, a Concordia farm girl who worked in Wichita's wartime aviation industry, in a civil ceremony in 1947. Like many "American" wives, Ruth Farha converted to the Orthodox faith and played an active role in church life. The community, in turn, embraced her—she joined the Lambda Sigs and later became president of the Bona Dea Club. (Courtesy Warren Farha.)

After World War II, the Blue Moon became a favorite spot for Lebanese socializing. Many first-generation Lebanese American couples enjoyed the prosperity of the 1950s by pursuing leisure and entertainment opportunities unthinkable to the hard-working immigrant generation. Couples returned home from such evenings with souvenir photographs in decorative club envelopes. (Above, courtesy Marlene Samra Orr and Kansas State Historical Society; below, courtesy Keith Stevens.)

Four

BEYOND DELANO

The decades after World War II altered the landscape of Wichita and ushered in a new era for the Arab Christian community. Wichita's Syrians began to call themselves "Lebanese," as they welcomed a fresh wave of immigrants from the newly independent nation of Lebanon. The mom-and-pop groceries founded in the 1920s and 1930s transitioned into modern supermarkets. Ever the entrepreneurs, Lebanese businessmen and women made their mark in the liquor trade, discount merchandising, electronics, oil exploration, nightclubs, car washes, and other emerging or expanding business fields. Meanwhile younger generations pursued higher education and began entering law, medicine, public service, and real estate. Although still tightly knit, the community gradually moved out of Delano and into newer, suburban-style neighborhoods in Riverside and East Wichita. While still excluded in some circles, charismatic Lebanese leaders emerged as political figures and philanthropists.

Bayouth and Samra children played on the Bayouth porch in Delano around 1942. The Syrian neighborhood in West Wichita promoted informal socializing among neighbors, much like village life in Lebanon. In the postwar decades, community members gradually dispersed to other parts of the city. Family gatherings remained important but socializing occurred more frequently now at church, or restaurants and nightclubs. (Courtesy Marlene Samra Orr and Kansas State Historical Society.)

One of the early families to leave Delano, the Ablahs built this Art Moderne-style duplex in 1939 in the fashionable Crown Heights neighborhood. Extended family living arrangements remained intact: Frank, wife Nellie, and children occupied one side of the duplex, brother Harvey and family the other, with a common room in the middle. "It was like growing up with four parents," a daughter recalled. (Photograph by Jay M. Price.)

Walt's Market continued the Lebanese family grocery tradition in its location at 914 East Harry Street. Alf Farha grew up helping his father behind the counter after school and on weekends. He estimated that Lebanese businessmen controlled over a quarter of Wichita's wholesale and retail grocery trade during the industry's heyday in the 1950s. (Courtesy Alfred Farha and Kansas State Historical Society.)

As the older generation retired, former groceries provided space for new ventures. A long-time clerk in her father's store, Lasema Kallail recognized the retail opportunities created by repeal of Kansas's dry laws in 1948. She opened her Kallail Liquor Store in the former family grocery on West Douglas Avenue. (Courtesy Kallail family and Kansas State Historical Society.)

Larger grocery chains modernized rapidly during the 1950s and 1960s. These smartly dressed cashiers worked in one of the Cut Rate Foods stores in 1955. The store's seven checkout stands were quite a novelty at the time. (Courtesy Howard Eastwood Collection, Special Collections and University Archives, Wichita State University Libraries.)

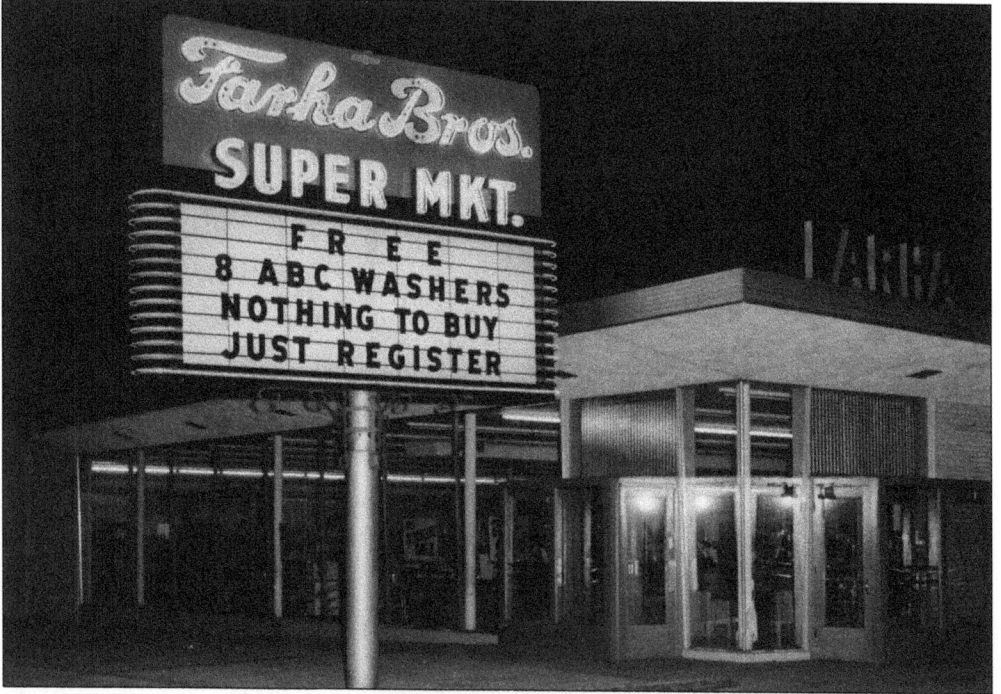

The Farha Brothers Super Markets had replaced the Cut Rate Foods stores by the early 1960s. Under this name, the family ultimately expanded its grocery business to nine locations. (Courtesy Wichita-Sedgwick County Historical Museum.)

This candid snapshot captured the five Farha brothers sharing a laugh in a family member's Riverside kitchen in 1954. William, Bahij, Philip, Sam, and LaBebe maintained close ties as their grocery empire grew. They also served in parish leadership roles at St. George Orthodox Church. (Courtesy Brenda Farha.)

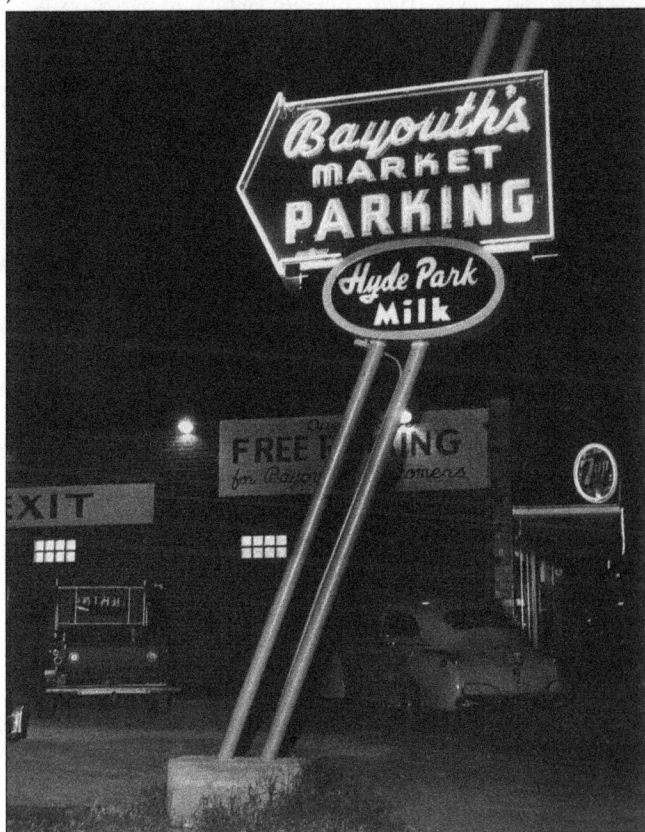

Another set of brothers, the sons of Ellis Bayouth, expanded their grocery store chain to multiple Wichita locations during this same time period. (Courtesy Wichita-Sedgwick County Historical Museum.)

A few Lebanese families owned modest entertainment venues before World War II. Tofey and Mary Haddad Steven (right) operated a billiard parlor on West Douglas in the late 1930s. While Wichita's Lebanese community largely adhered to the Orthodox Christian faith, the Steven family was part of a small Roman Catholic minority. (Courtesy Joe and Esther Steven.)

Another branch of the Steven family ran dance clubs that entertained aviation workers during Wichita's booming 1940s. One such venue was the Plamor. (Courtesy Joe and Esther Steven.)

The postwar boom attracted other Lebanese entrepreneurs to the nightclub business, where they served both Lebanese and non-Lebanese clienteles. Al Steven, on the right with his bartenders, operated the Hi Ho. Jimmy Razook and Taft Stephan ran the Flamingo while Freddie Ferris established Freddie's Brass Rail. (Courtesy Lindy Andeel.)

Young men returning from war learned new trades quickly. George Jabara, left, ran a construction company that built housing for aircraft workers in south Wichita. Brother-in-law Jim Bayouth, center, moved into the printing business, relying on relatives and paper salesmen to teach him the ropes. Frank Jabara, right, became a supermarket butcher. (Courtesy Michael and Julia Bayouth.)

In the 1950s, Ken "Curley" Razook went into the furniture business with his brothers. From a store in north Wichita, the venture expanded to six locations across the city, including this branch that the family opened in 1973 on East Douglas Avenue. Ken's son, Bob, kept this store going after his father's retirement in 1980. (Photograph by Jay M. Price.)

After David Stevens's death in 1949, nephew Keeney transformed the family's wholesale candy and tobacco company into one of the first discount houses in the country. Keeney's West City sold everything from televisions and toasters to watches and jewelry. (Courtesy Keith Stevens.)

Department stores included children's sections, but Camal (Kay) Aboussie became one of the first Wichita retailers devoted exclusively to children's clothing. His establishment, called Cradle Land, opened its doors in 1947 at 125 North Broadway. Aboussie is on the left, with Manira Aboussie (center) and a woman salesclerk. (Courtesy Betty Aboussie Ellis.)

Lizzie Henry's son launched his Gene Henry Television in the storefront previously occupied by the family grocery. The business provided sales and repair service for the newest American consumer sensation. (Photograph by *Wichita Eagle*, courtesy Thomas Laham.)

George and Lorraine Husson Ferris sold electronics from their Ka-Lo Store in Hutchinson during the 1950s. The couple later returned to Wichita and opened an amusement park called Frontier Village. They followed that venture with a restaurant and bakery. (Courtesy Lorraine Ferris and Kansas State Historical Society.)

Fred Ayesh dropped out of high school to work for Ablah Hotel Supply during the Depression. After the war, he became an oilman. With his brother Richard, he founded two companies, Zetco and Paramount, which leased drilling rights as far west as Wyoming. This rig drilled for an Ayesh project in Elk County, Kansas. (Courtesy Richard Ayesh.)

One of the Ablah Hotel Supply Company's ventures included a fleet of small, portable metal diners. During World War II, salesman Arthur Valentine took over that part of the business, establishing himself as an early developer of prefabricated metal buildings. He marketed the Ablah design as the Valentine Diner. A relative of the Ablahs utilized some of these diners in his business in Oklahoma City. (Above, courtesy Amil Ablah; below, courtesy Lindy Andeel.)

Several Lebanese individuals became particularly successful in real estate. Phil Ruffin (the name was anglicized from Rufan, and his mother was a Cohlmia) began his career developing 7-11 convenience stores. In time, he became one of Wichita's most successful real estate figures whose ventures included the Wichita Greyhound Park. (Courtesy Special Collections and University Archives, Wichita State University Libraries.)

Their early start with Ablah Hotel Supply inspired brothers Don and George Ablah to enter real estate. George (center, with wife Virginia) was a driving force behind the development of north Wichita, especially the commercial ventures along Rock Road. In time, George joined with Charles Koch to form the real estate investment company ABKO. (Courtesy Lindy Andeel.)

Lebanese families kept up the tradition of training their children in the art of entrepreneurship. Each of the 11 children of Joe and Esther Steven in this converted bus, used for family excursions, went on to found businesses of their own. (Photograph by *Wichita Eagle*, courtesy Joe and Esther Steven.)

The first major Steven venture was Joe's Seat Cover and Car Wash, introducing "brushless" technology to Wichita car owners in 1954. This car wash on Seneca was the first of a series of car washes that Joe and several of his children ran. (Courtesy Joe and Esther Steven.)

The Bona Dea Club, its coveted membership slots limited to 35 women, celebrated a quarter century in 1966. Club members played a leading role in Lebanese community life. They organized the annual Labor Day celebrations with a sister club in Oklahoma City, which hosted the event in alternate years. The club supported charities as well, raising $30,000 in 1977 to assist residents of war-ravaged Lebanon. (Courtesy Bona Dea Club.)

BENEFIT DINNER
LADIES OF ST. GEORGE CHURCH

LEBANESE DINNER

SERVED AT
ST. GEORGE EDUCATIONAL BUILDING

SUNDAY, OCTOBER 16, 1966

12:30 Till 3:00 p. m.   5:00 Till 8:00 p. m.

210 SOUTH WALNUT $2.50 Per Person

The annual Lebanese dinners at St. George had become a Wichita institution by the 1960s. In 1973, churchwomen prepared meals of kibbe, talemy bread, yabra, ruz (rice), yaknee (green bean-tomato stew), and baklawa (pastry dessert) for some 1,500 diners in the parish hall. (Courtesy St. George Orthodox Cathedral.)

In the days leading up to the 1973 St. Mary Food Fair, Julia Yanney prepared fatayer (meat pies) according to a Lebanese family recipe. Meanwhile Joan Kamas and Lorraine Kallail (below) loaded a tray with fresh-baked spinach fatayer in preparation for the big event. Other St. Mary specialties included kibbe, cabbage rolls, green beans, tabouli salad, and baklawa. (Photographs by *Wichita Eagle*, courtesy Kallail family.)

Col. James Jabara (shown with his wife, Nina, and children) began his career as a fighter ace during World War II, receiving the Distinguished Flying Cross. In the Korean Conflict, he flew the F-86 Sabre, becoming the nation's first jet ace. He returned home to a hero's welcome and a nationwide publicity campaign that included this parade in Wichita. Jabara remains one of Wichita's best-known Lebanese figures. In 1980, the city named its general aviation airport the Colonel James Jabara Airport in his honor. (Above, courtesy Wichita-Sedgwick County Historical Museum; below, courtesy Richard Ayesh.)

Controversial and colorful,
John Stevens started in the
vending machine business and
then entered local politics as a
conservative Republican. He
served as city commissioner
from 1963 to 1966, as mayor
from 1966 to 1967, and again as
commissioner from 1969 until his
death in 1976. His sometimes-
confrontational approach
contributed to the "Tuesday
Night Fights" in the commission
chambers. The cartoon is
from the *Wichita Eagle-Beacon*.
(Courtesy Keith Stevens.)

The son of grocer Taft Stephan, Robert
Stephan began his public service career as a
Wichita municipal judge. Elected to the state
attorney general's office in 1979, he became
one of the most popular state officials in
recent history, serving four consecutive
terms. (Courtesy Robert and Don Stephan.)

One of Wichita's earliest Lebanese physicians, Alex Laham specialized in internal medicine. His family gathered proudly for his graduation from medical school at the University of Kansas in 1943. Dr. Laham practiced in Wichita for many years. (Courtesy Thomas Laham.)

Accounting professor Fran Jabara helped create Wichita State University's Center for Entrepreneurship in 1977. Later on, as head of Jabara Ventures Group, he continued to mentor local entrepreneurs, including restaurateur—and close friend—Antoine Toubia. (Courtesy Special Collections and University Archives, Wichita State University Libraries.)

George Farha (seen at right in his native Beirut) represented the new wave of Lebanese immigrants pursuing professional careers in America. After earning his medical degree from Tulane, Farha practiced surgery in Wichita with his brother Jim. When they retired in 1998 (below), their practice had grown to 25 surgeons. Dr. Farha became a leading Lebanese philanthropist, chairing a million-dollar campaign for Wichita State University athletics and endowing the George J. Farha Library at the University of Kansas School of Medicine in Wichita. His decades of service to the Orthodox Church earned him national and international respect. (Courtesy Dr. George and Brenda Farha.)

Interested in supporting higher education, the Ablahs gave their Colorado-Derby building, already filled with paying tenants, to the university to finance construction of a new library. Only after considerable pressure from the university did the family allow the new facility to be named Ablah Library. (Courtesy Special Collections and University Archives, Wichita State University Libraries.)

Walid Gholmieh, one of the most prominent composers and conductors in the Arab world, received an honorary master of music degree from Wichita State University in 1974. Although a link between the university and the Baalbek International Festival in Lebanon never fully developed, Gholmieh's ties to Wichita continued. His brother's family later immigrated to Wichita. (Courtesy Special Collections and University Archives, Wichita State University Libraries.)

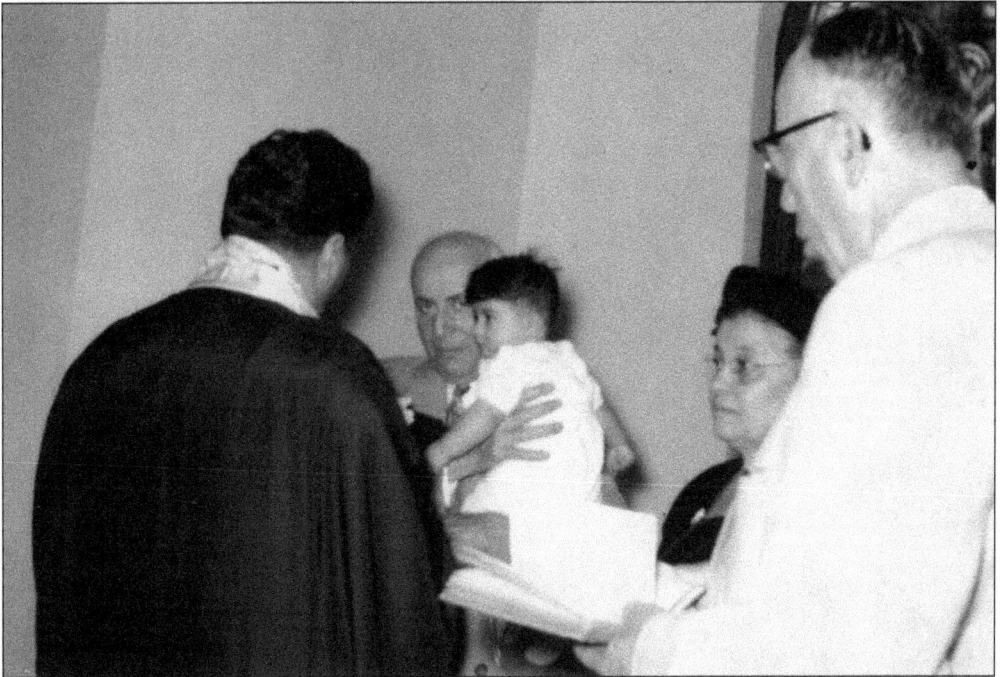

The baby boom helped usher the second and third generations into Wichita's Lebanese community. Fr. Michael Husson presided at the St. Mary Church baptism of Ken Kallail, with E. G. Stevens and Nora Salome serving as sponsors, and parish president Frank Stevens assisting as chanter. (Courtesy Kallail family.)

Godmother Edna Saleme held Gayle Farha as Fr. John Matthiesen administered the sacrament of baptism in 1961 at St. George. Mother Brenda Farha (right) and daughter Gayle both consider themselves first generation Lebanese Americans; Gayle's father, George, as well as Brenda's father, Bahij Farha, were born in Lebanon. (Courtesy Tiffany Farha.)

At the 2007 wedding reception of Jasmin Steven and John Rupe, guests danced the traditional Lebanese dubke. A lively group dance, the dubke is a popular part of many Lebanese parties and social gatherings. The vast majority of wedding celebrations in the Lebanese community today include the dubke, regardless of whether the couple represents the first or fourth generation in America. At left is a *dirbukka* (dumbek) played to accompany Lebanese dances in Wichita since the 1940s. (Above, courtesy Jasmin Steven Rupe; left, courtesy Bona Dea Club.)

Five

UPHOLDING TRADITION, EMBRACING CHANGE

In recent decades, the Lebanese community has experienced both change and continuity. Patriarchs and matriarchs from the postwar years gave way to younger generations who moved into the professions or took the reins of family businesses. Unrest in Lebanon resulted in a new wave of immigrants since the late 1970s. Some were professionals, while others became prominent local restaurateurs, establishing in Wichita a remarkable tradition of Mediterranean cuisine. Long-time families who had been used to home cooking or importing Lebanese foodstuffs marveled that they could now get hummus, pita bread, and shawarmah from restaurants. Meanwhile St. George and St. Mary churches started attracting non-Lebanese converts who were drawn to Orthodox Christianity's profound theology, mystical tradition, and rich liturgy. After contributing to the fabric of Wichita life for over a century, the Lebanese now enjoy widespread recognition for the role they have played in the city's history.

Those who came of age in the postwar years continued the tradition of small-scale mercantiles. Farris Farha's connections to the grocery business led him to food distribution for the Wichita-based franchise Pizza Hut. In the 1970s, Farha became a Pizza Hut vice president. In recent years, however, he returned to the family's tradition of entrepreneurship by establishing the Farris Wheel candy store adjacent to Toubia's Piccadilly Market and Grill. (Photograph by Jay M. Price.)

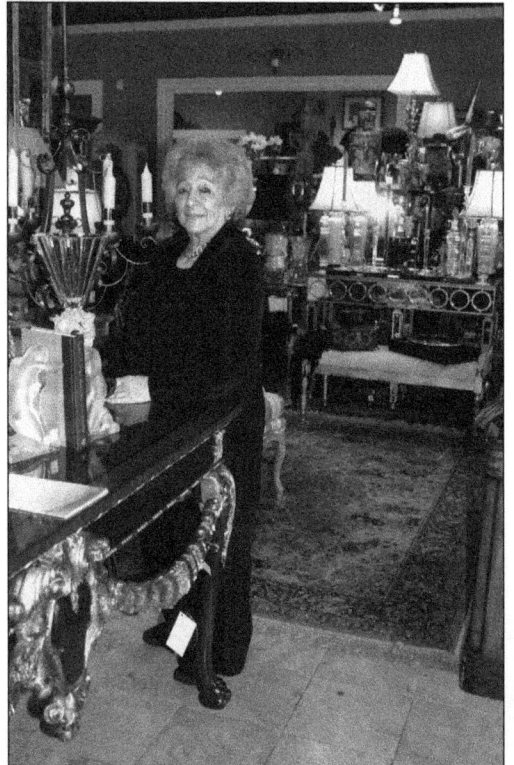

Helen Jabara Galloway and her sister Donna Jabara Baker went into business together, opening The First Place in 1973. Inspired by the example of customer service set by their father, Farris Jabara, Helen insists on similar attention to customer needs in the upscale store. (Photograph by Jay M. Price.)

Ray Sales, the last of the downtown Lebanese groceries, continues to serve customers in the city's core. Owner Ray Farha began his wholesale operation "peddling" out of the back of his truck in the early 1960s. His grocery store, two blocks north of the new downtown arena, dates to 1975. Farha's two daughters and son-in-law work in the family store, mirroring the Lebanese groceries of a century ago. (Photograph by Jay M. Price.)

As the years passed, family businesses continued over the generations. George Jabara's business handling damaged freight and flooring remnants from the mobile home industry developed into Jabara's Carpet Galerie and Jabara's Carpet Outlet. His son Tom continues the business with the help of family members. (Photograph by Jay M. Price.)

Dale and Craig Steven expanded the menu and offerings of their fast food Coney Island restaurants in the 1980s. A 1984 contest resulted in a new name for the restaurant chain, and Spangles became a Wichita icon. Today the company operates around two dozen 1950s diner–themed restaurants in Wichita, Topeka, and across central Kansas. Spangles introduced pita bread and gyros to the local fast food market long before they became fashionable with mainstream chains. (Courtesy Spangles.)

Jim Elkouri's modest grocery provided the work ethic that drove son David to co-found the nationally respected Hinkle Elkouri Law Firm with the help of longtime friend and colleague Eric Namee. Located on the top floors of the Epic Center and in Wilson Estates, the firm is the second largest in Wichita and represents many Lebanese-owned businesses, as well as prestigious clients around the country. (Courtesy Debbi Elkouri.)

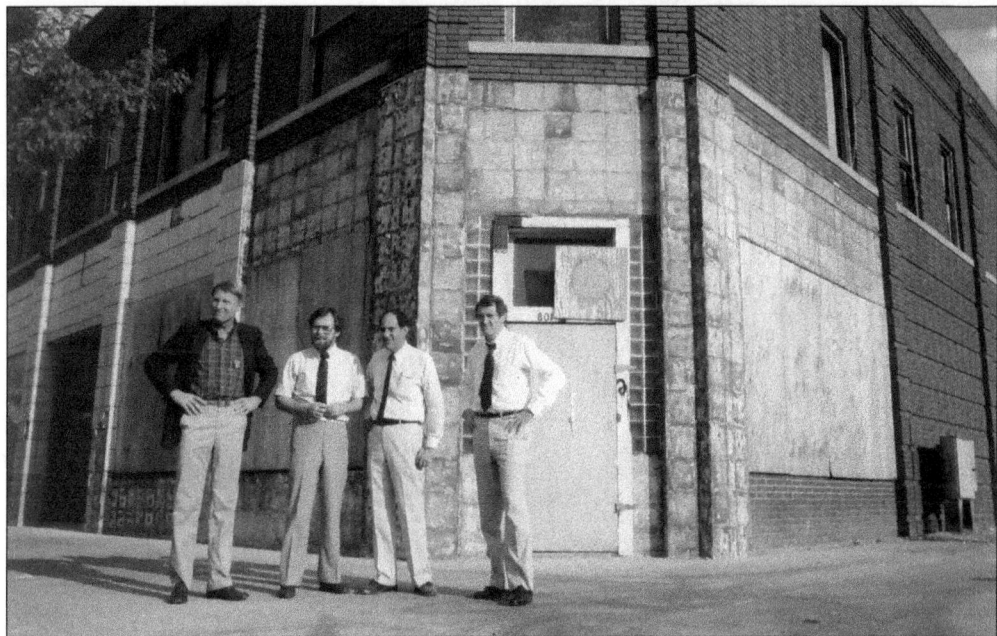

Downtown developer Keith Stevens (second from right) facilitated the transformation of the original Bayouth Printing Company into part of the new headquarters for major advertising firm Sullivan Higdon & Sink. (Courtesy Sullivan Higdon & Sink.)

George Laham II began his career in real estate while still a student at the University of Kansas. Returning to Wichita, he proved himself to be a visionary realtor with his upscale Bradley Fair shopping center development on Rock Road. (Photograph by Quigg Studios, courtesy Bradley Fair.)

Wichita's strong Lebanese community draws other Lebanese Americans looking for places to settle. A native of Peoria, Illinois, Susan Peters came to Wichita in 1983 to anchor KWCH-TV news, later joining KAKE-TV. Proud of her Lebanese heritage, she came to Wichita in part because she knew there was a supportive Lebanese presence. (Courtesy KAKE-TV.)

Brandon Steven and Rodney Steven II are the next generation to follow that family's business tradition. In 1994, 22-year-old Rodney launched Genesis Health Clubs, a physical fitness facility with four locations and a partnership with Via Christi Medical Center. Brother Brandon, meanwhile, established Brandon Steven Motors near this Genesis on Rock Road. (Photograph by Jay M. Price.)

In the mid-1970s, Arab-Israeli tensions spilled into southern Lebanon, including Jedeidat Marjeyoun (above). Meanwhile, the 15-year Lebanese Civil War, waged primarily between Maronites and Shiite Muslims, devastated Beirut. The inhabitants of once-peaceful villages witnessed bombs and shellings from the porches of their homes, dodged occasional gunfire, and struggled to maintain everyday life amid the complete disruption of economic and social services. These conflicts led Lebanese, especially Christians, to emigrate. The remnants of the violence remain visible today. (Both photographs by Chris Razook.)

A teenager during the Lebanese Civil War, Sam Cohlmia left his native Beirut for Los Angeles and Wichita, where the family had relatives. After graduating from Wichita State University and the University of Kansas School of Medicine, he practiced in the 1990s in Lebanon before starting his Wichita ophthalmology practice. As head chanter at St. George Cathedral, Dr. Cohlmia carries on family tradition: his father and uncle both chanted at St. George. (Courtesy Dr. Sam Cohlmia.)

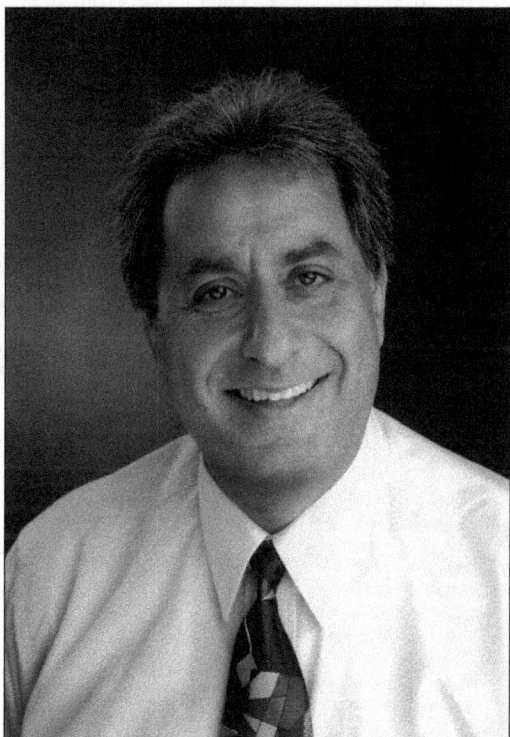

With roots in Jedeidat Marjeyoun, oncologist Shaker Dakhil attended medical school in Beirut and went to Wayne State University for his residency. Established in Wichita in 1981, he became one of the region's leading cancer specialists. His Cancer Center of Kansas has attracted other medical figures to the city, including several of Lebanese background. (Photograph by Via Christi Photograph Department, courtesy Dr. Shaker Dakhil.)

The Antoine Toubia family originally came from Dair Mamas, near Jedeidat Marjeyoun, but relocated to Beirut in the 1950s. After coming to Wichita, Toubia established the Olive Tree in 1979. An innovative and upscale restaurant, the Olive Tree introduced Wichitans to a host of French and Middle Eastern foods, from fresh salmon to fattouch salad. The family's LaTour company went on to operate the Faculty Club at Wichita State, the Café Chantilly, and the grocery store–restaurant Piccadilly. LaTour was a family affair, including sister Gracia, brother Naji, and, seen below, sisters Joumana and Randa. (Above, photograph by Les Broadstreet and courtesy *Wichita Eagle*; below, photograph by Jay M. Price.)

In the late 1970s, the Steven family brought their relative Melad Stephan to Wichita. In Lebanon, Stephan grew up around the food industry, with a father who handled food service for airlines in the Middle East. Stephan founded his own set of restaurants, including Nouvelle Café on Rock Road as well as the Old Town restaurants Uptown Bistro, Egg Cetera, the Latin American–themed Sabor, and Oeno Wine Bar. (Courtesy Jay M. Price.)

Like N. F. Farha and E. G. Stevens decades earlier, Antoine Toubia and Melad Stephan brought their countrymen to Wichita. When importing pita bread became costly, Toubia brought in Lebanese-born baker John Srour from Detroit. Srour founded N&J (Naji and John) bakery with Naji Toubia. Since then, Naji went on to found his own bakery, Bagatelle, while N&J now includes a restaurant of its own. (Photograph by Jay M. Price.)

Tony Abdayem fled the civil war in Lebanon, went to WSU, and worked at Bagatelle. With the help of family, including wife Michelene and daughter Samantha (left), he started La Galette in 1986. Located on West Douglas, within sight of buildings that once housed Wichita's original Lebanese businesses, La Galette specializes in French as well as Lebanese items. (Photograph by Jay M. Price.)

Wichita State University programs have attracted
large numbers of international students, including
Muslims from Lebanon. Among them were
brothers Mike, Ali, and Ty Issa. Mike (shown
here at his wedding in Lebanon) and family
founded the Italian Garden Ristorante in 1988.
Ty established the upscale Larkspur in Old Town.
The family has recently expanded its ventures to
include a hookah bar. (Courtesy Lindy Andeel.)

Lebanese Muslim Ali Ibrahim came to Wichita to attend Wichita State University. After
graduation, he acquired M.I.F. Deli (Mediterranean International Foods) from the David
family. Sons Nadim and Wassim, seated at the deli booth, want to pursue careers in medicine.
(Photograph by Jay M. Price.)

As political stability permits, Wichita's current generation of Lebanese immigrants makes periodic trips home to see friends and relatives. In 2000, Dr. Sam Cohlmia visited Koura, in the heart of the Orthodox Christian region of northern Lebanon, staying with friends near Bishmizzeen. (Courtesy Dr. Sam Cohlmia.)

Randa Haddad moved to Wichita from Lebanon via Damascus in the 1980s, part of the more recent wave of immigration from the region. She maintained close ties to her homeland even as other family members joined her in Kansas. She traveled to the Syrian monastery of Saidnaya for the baptism of her son, Gabriel Stevens. (Courtesy Randa Haddad Stevens and Kansas State Historical Society.)

For the descendants of the earlier Lebanese immigrants, visits to the old country involved places and families that previously had existed only through the stories that their grandparents told. During a recent trip to Jedeidat Marjeyoun, the Razooks visited the small structure that had been the original family homestead. The tranquility of this village of about 2,000 people belied the turbulence of recent years. (Photograph by Chris Razook.)

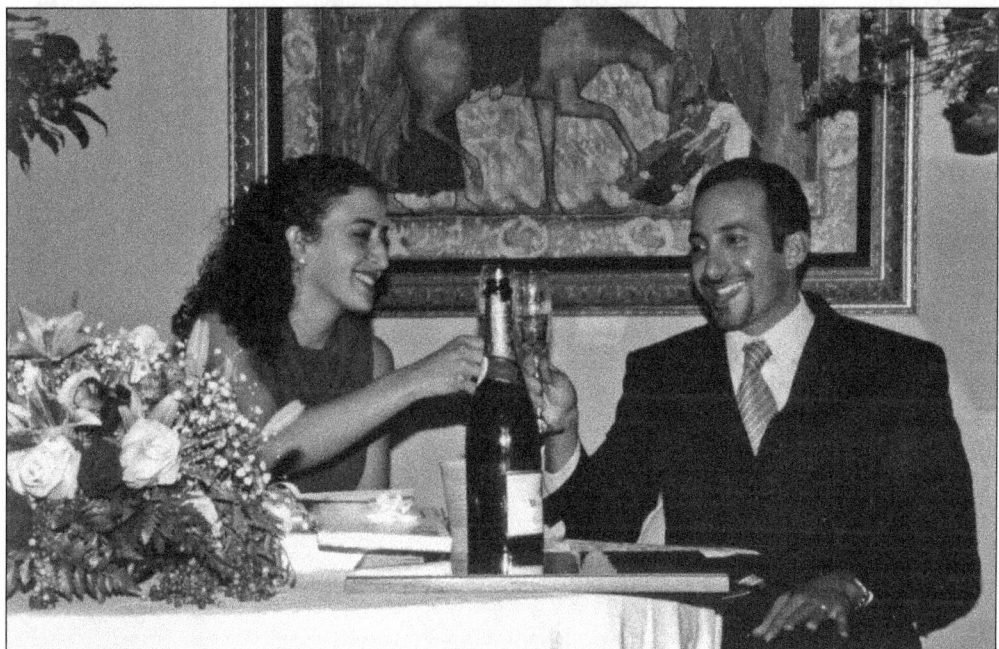

James Shadid, youth director (and now assistant priest) at St. George, celebrated his 2002 marriage to Gizelle Baba, the daughter of Palestinian Christian immigrants. An Oklahoman, he grew up conversant in Arabic and received part of his seminary training in Lebanon. Ordained in 2004, Father James is a grandson of Fr. Nayemtallah Shadid, whose brother, Fr. Shukrallah, had close ties to Wichita. (Courtesy St. George Orthodox Cathedral.)

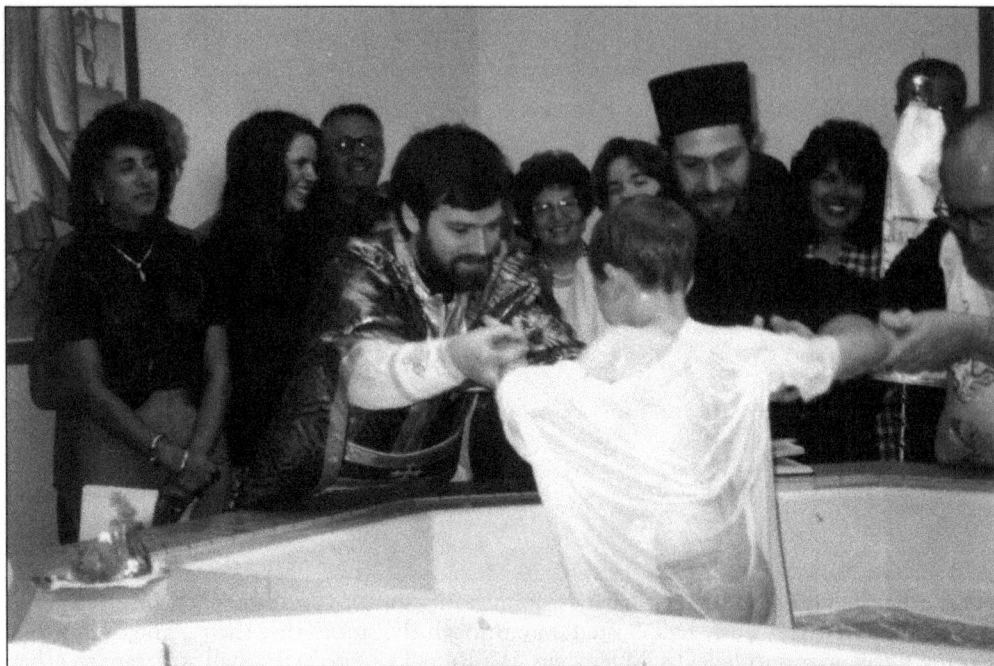

Adult and youth baptisms, such as this one, occurred more frequently in recent years as the church welcomed a steady stream of converts from secular backgrounds and other faith traditions. Converts from Christian denominations typically enter the church through the sacrament of chrismation, or anointing, rather than baptism. (Courtesy St. George Orthodox Cathedral.)

These altar boys, representing the youngest members of the St. George Orthodox community, reflect the parish's growing diversity. (Courtesy St. George Orthodox Cathedral.)

In spite of changing demographics and new generations coming of age, cultural traditions remain. Even if they no longer consume traditional Lebanese foods on a daily basis, families incorporate them into celebrations, weddings, and baptisms. Thelma Namee, Lorraine Ferris, and Nina Busada prepared kibbe, a delicacy made from raw ground lamb or beef, for the wedding of Eric Namee and Tracy Ferris. (Courtesy Sadie Namee and Kansas State Historical Society.)

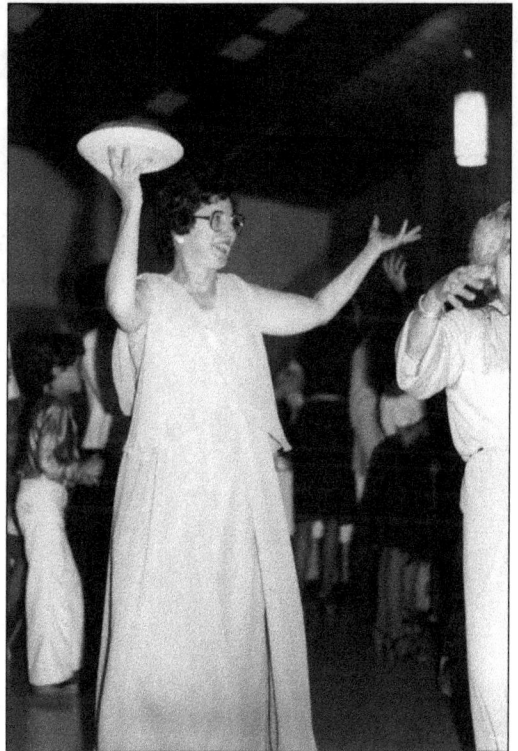

Sadie Namee enters her son's wedding reception bearing a platter of raw kibbe (kibbe nayeh). Traditionally relatives present a platter of kibbe to the newlyweds in an elaborate dance procession, complete with Arabic music. (Courtesy Eric and Tracy Namee.)

Parts of the Orthodox marriage ceremony date to the sixth century. Fr. Jason Del Vitto exchanged the wedding crowns over the heads of Eric and Tracy Namee during their 1980 wedding. Today the bride or groom may be non-Lebanese, but the ceremony remains the same. (Courtesy Eric and Tracy Namee.)

The annual Lebanese food bazaar at St. Mary has been among the most popular local community events. (Above, photograph by *Wichita Eagle*, courtesy Kallail family; below, photograph by Jay M. Price)

Marguerite Farha (left), Jacque Kouri, Katie Elkouri, Judy Hull, Eva Pappas, and Vivianne Farha work in the kitchen preparing the St. George dinner. Although the dinner takes place in October, cooking preparation begins months in advance. (Courtesy St. George Orthodox Cathedral.)

Amare Selassie and Hank Farha are among the men who assisted at the 75th annual St. George Lebanese Dinner in 2008, which served nearly 6,000 meals. The dinner today involves both young and old, with tasks ranging from directing parking to serving tables, preparing carry-out, selling packaged pastries, and leading church tours. (Photograph by Jay M. Price.)

The Lebanese have become active contributors to civic and community events across Wichita. In this case, the members of St. Mary staffed a 1997 booth as part of the city's biggest celebration, Riverfest. (Courtesy Rosemary Kallail and Kansas State Historical Society.)

The Steven family started a long-standing Wichita tradition with their extensive Christmas decorations, first on their family business and later at home. Intended originally for their own children and grandchildren, the displays attracted thousands of visitors from around the city every year. (Courtesy Joe and Esther Steven.)

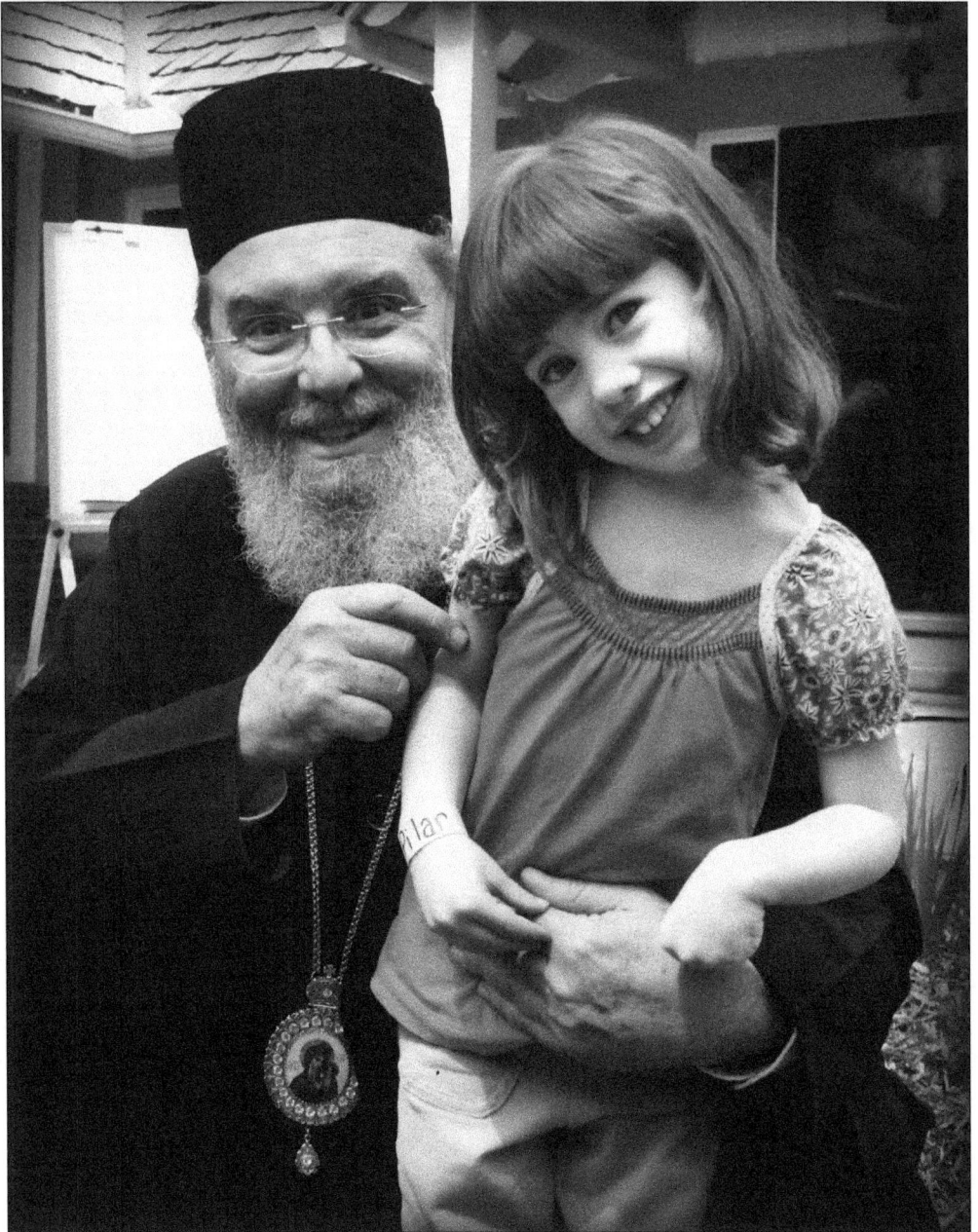

Orthodox Christians end their annual Lenten fast with Lazarus Saturday, which commemorates Jesus' raising of Lazarus from the tomb. Each year, Bishop Basil hosts a Lazarus Saturday children's festival on the chancery grounds that features pony rides, egg hunts, and arts and crafts booths. Children from Orthodox parishes across Kansas look forward to their special day and the opportunity to express their love for "Saidna" (an affectionate Arabic term for bishop). (Photograph by Ze Bernardinello.)

The child-centered character of Lazarus Saturday carries over to Palm Sunday, celebrated the following day. Fourth-century pilgrims in Jerusalem reported children participating in Palm Sunday processions, a tradition maintained 17 centuries later by Arab Orthodox Christians around the world. At St. Mary, children of all ages carry sha'aneenes (branches hung with candy) in the outdoor procession. (Courtesy Rosemary Kallail and Kansas State Historical Society.)

Dr. Jim Farha's young children carry their candles to church in preparation for St. George's Palm Sunday procession in 1970. (Courtesy Tiffany Farha.)

Led by the priests, bishop, and altar servers, St. George parishioners bearing palm fronds prepare to exit the church on Palm Sunday. After everyone circles the temple, the children gather around the bishop and shout "Hosanna!" on cue during his reading of the Palm Sunday gospel. (Photographs by Doug Wereb.)

During the Great and Holy Friday service, a cloth icon representing Christ's crucified body is placed in a wooden bier decorated with flowers. Representing mourners at a funeral service, parishioners follow the bier in an evening procession around the church. As worshippers re-enter the narthex, they pass beneath the bier, which symbolizes their entry into life in Christ through His death and burial. (Photograph by Jay M. Price.)

Pascha (Easter) begins at midnight in a darkened church. Gradually the light of candles, symbolizing the Resurrection, fills the space with a warm glow. The greeting "Christ is risen! Indeed He is risen!" marks the beginning of the most joyous season of the Orthodox year. (Photograph by Doug Wereb.)

St. Mary parishioners carry on the old Lebanese village tradition of making Pascha "rounds." On Easter Sunday morning, after resting up from the midnight services at church, parishioners go from home to home enjoying festive foods and hospitality. Families engage in a friendly competition to see who can offer the finest delicacies and the most decorative tables. (Courtesy Rosemary Kallail and Kansas State Historical Society.)

During the Pascha rounds, St. Mary families always visit the home of Evelyn Ferris in Delano. This house is one of the few original homes in the old Lebanese neighborhood still occupied by a community member. (Courtesy Eric and Tracy Namee.)

From 1948 to 1989, St. George parishioners worshipped in their second church on South Walnut Street in Delano. The congregation constructed its third and present house of worship on 13th Street near Rock Road in 1990. The following year, St. George was elevated to the status of cathedral. In 2004, it became the seat of the Diocese of Wichita and Mid-America, one of only nine Antiochian Orthodox dioceses in North America. Elaborate iconography adorns the ceiling and walls, including this Christ Pantocrator (Almighty) in the dome. (Above, photograph by Jay M. Price; below, photograph by Doug Wereb.)

In 1992, Fr. Basil Essey, pastor of St. George Cathedral, was elevated to the rank of bishop by the Holy Synod of the Greek Orthodox Patriarchate of the Great City-of-God Antioch and all the East. Above, Father Basil reads the ancient confession of faith; below, his fellow bishops lead him around the altar in the Dance of Isaiah. In 2004, he became the first diocesan bishop of the newly created Diocese of Wichita and Mid-America. Bishop Basil is one of the best-known Orthodox hierarchs in America, overseeing 50 parishes in nine states. (Photographs by Larry Fleming, courtesy Rt. Rev. Basil Essey.)

Wichita's Lebanese community took great pride in watching two of its young men enter the priesthood in the 21st century. In 2001, Bishop Basil ordained Fr. Michael Shanbour, son of Mitch and Linda Shadid Shanbour. He now serves a parish in Spokane, Washington. Father Michael is a great-grandson of Fr. Shukrallah Shadid, the visiting priest at St. George during the community's formative years of the early 1920s. (Courtesy St. George Orthodox Cathedral.)

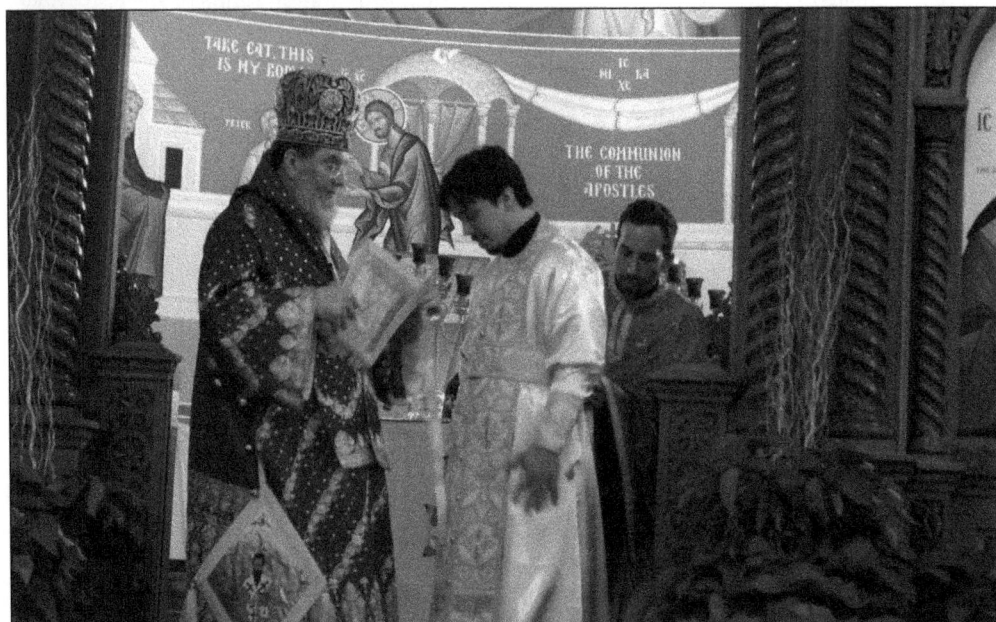

Isaac Farha, son of Glen and Valerie Farha and great-grandson of immigrant N. S. Farha, became skilled in Byzantine chant while still in high school and later attended St. Tikhon's Seminary. Bishop Basil blesses Father Isaac's priestly vestments at his 2007 ordination while Father James assists. Father Isaac and Khouriya Anastasia ("khouriya" is an Arabic honorific for "priest's wife") serve a parish in her native Alaska. (Photograph by Sid Edgmon.)

The influence of local Orthodox churches extends well beyond Wichita. St. Mary has sent teams to Project Mexico (above) to build homes for poor residents of Tijuana, while other volunteers assisted at St. Innocent Orphanage. Both churches support Native Alaskan seminarians through Outreach Alaska; Hogar Rafael Ayau, an Orthodox orphanage in Guatemala; and a substance abuse program in Romania initiated by a former Wichitan. (Courtesy Eric and Tracy Namee.)

In Africa, Orthodox Christians must often walk miles to reach the nearest Orthodox church. St. George Cathedral raised the $20,000 needed to build this village church for a parish in Ghana. Africans searching for an ancient Christianity, with no ties to the continent's colonial past, have been responsible for Orthodoxy's rapid spread in recent decades. (Courtesy St. George Orthodox Cathedral.)

The parishes of St. George and St. Mary created the Treehouse in 2001. Its programs support new mothers who carry their babies to term under difficult circumstances. In 2008, members of the Najim family gathered with Treehouse director Renee Croitoru and Fr. Paul O'Callaghan for the dedication of the Jamelia Najim Center for Moms and Babies. (Photograph by Michael Croitoru, courtesy the Treehouse.)

Based in Wichita, the nonprofit Virginia H. Farah Foundation dedicates its funds exclusively to the work of the Orthodox Church. Its national and international grant recipients engage in all areas of church life, from humanitarian efforts and missionary labor to education and scholarly work. Board members Bruce Ferris, Eric Namee, and Valerie Ferris DeBolt discuss grants. (Photograph by Jay M. Price.)

After six decades, the Bona Dea Club still meets regularly. The last Labor Day dance occurred around 2000, but club members continue to publish a directory of Wichita's Lebanese community every few years, carrying on the tradition started by the Al-pha Club in 1938. In 2001, club members and spouses gathered for a Christmas celebration. (Courtesy Bona Dea Club.)

Extended family gatherings continue to be a hallmark of Wichita's Lebanese community. The Kallails of Wichita gathered at Christmas in 1991, while the Farha family reunions, like this one in 1985, attract dozens of relatives from around the country. (Above courtesy Rosemary Kallail and Kansas State Historical Society; below, courtesy Alfred Farha and Kansas State Historical Society.)

The Lebanese peddling tradition comes full circle with Eighth Day Books founder Warren Farha, who sells classics in history, religion, and literature at book fairs as well as from his Wichita store. "The only difference between me and my grandfather is that I drive a van and he drove a wagon," Farha said. Son Timothy takes his peddling into cyberspace, marketing hookahs on the Internet. (Photograph by Jay M. Price.)

Visit us at
arcadiapublishing.com

www.ingramcontent.com/pod-product-compliance
Lightning Source LLC
Chambersburg PA
CBHW050612110426
42813CB00008B/2532